Religion in Focu

Christianity

in today's world

Teacher's Resource Book

Claire Clinton

Sally Lynch

Janet Orchard

Deborah Weston

Angela Wright

Faith community editor

Sally Lynch

John Murray

Other titles in this series:

Islam in today's world Student's Book ISBN 0 7195 7194 4
Teacher's Resource Book ISBN 0 7195 7432 3
Judaism in today's world Student's Book ISBN 0 7195 7197 9
Teacher's Resource Book ISBN 0 7195 7433 1

Acknowledgements

The authors and publishers are grateful to the following for permission to include material in this book:
p.102 © Jostein Gaarder from *Sophie's World*, Orion Publishing Group;
p.68 © David Hare 1996.

While every effort has been made to contact copyright holders, the publishers apologise for any omissions, which they will be pleased to rectify at the earliest opportunity.

Examination questions are reproduced by kind permission of the Midland Examining Group (**pp.66, 91, 124** and **125**) and The Northern Examinations and Assessment Board (**pp.24, 43, 49, 74, 77, 96** and **114**).

© Claire Clinton, Sally Lynch, Janet Orchard, Deborah Weston, Angela Wright

First published 1998
by John Murray (Publishers) Ltd
50 Albemarle Street
London W1X 4BD

Layouts by Amanda Hawkes.
Illustrations by Oxford Illustrators Ltd.
Cover design by John Townson/Creation.
Typeset in 10/12pt Rockwell Light by Wearset, Boldon, Tyne and Wear.
Printed in Great Britain by St Edmundsbury Press, Bury St Edmunds.

A CIP record for this publication is available from the British Library

ISBN 0 7195 7431 5
Student's Book ISBN 0 7195 7193 6

Contents

Introduction

What is the value of Religious Education?

The authors of this book were all involved with the development and approval of the GCSE short course RE syllabuses. We believe that the courses which have emerged give RE a most valuable and exciting place in students' all-round education – they help make RE as relevant to all students today as it has ever been.

The practical importance of GCSE accreditation to the future of Key Stage 4 RE is obvious to all. What has been perhaps less emphasised is the opportunity opened up by the new courses to discover the deeper value of RE to the growth and development of the student.

A personal journey

One central aim of RE is to help students to see their way through the cloudy and difficult path that we call the journey of life. The 'way' may well be different for each person, but the best method of finding it is for our students to think for themselves about ultimate questions of meaning and value rather than to simply accept the values and beliefs of others.

It is this personal journey that can make RE so different from RS. RE is not just the academic study of phenomena associated with religions, it is a study which involves the students themselves, asking them to make a response to religious concepts, beliefs and values. On such a personal journey, to some extent, there are no right or wrong answers.

In-depth investigation

However, RE is more than a personal journey – it is also an in-depth investigation of a complex set of beliefs and values.

One aim of this course is to help students to see beyond the stereotypical Christianity sometimes portrayed in the media (and even in RE lessons) which can too easily present an ill-informed or misleading account.

Through this course students investigate and respond to Christian beliefs about moral and theological issues. Other books in the series investigate other world religions in a similar way.

The value of RE is increased greatly if students study a topic in depth. This produces higher quality work from all students and an appropriate challenge for all abilities – it allows access to all while also stretching the very highest attainers.

Thinking skills

John Scully, former Chief Executive of Apple Computers, has said: 'we should be preparing students for jobs of the future, jobs that will require thinking skills, not rote memorisation and repetition'. Yet current educational research suggests that only about 20 per cent of our GCSE level students can use complex thinking skills. The 80 per cent majority are poor at empathising; they jump to conclusions; have difficulty with abstract or generalised solutions to problems; can't accept that there may be more than one answer to a problem; they see their lives and the world around them in black and white rather than in shades of grey. The risk is that the time pressures of the prescribed curriculum deepen this problem early in the school, turning students into surface learners.

The GCSE years are a key time to make this transition to higher-order thinking skills. And RE is a good vehicle through which to do it. In this course, particularly in studying the issues of morality and in the philosophy and theology of Unit 5, students learn to generalise; abstract; analyse; classify; contrast; reframe ideas and communicate conclusions in a wide variety of contexts. RE requires work with concepts which no other subject on the curriculum demands.

RE also develops understanding of people. The skills required for exploring other people's values and beliefs make short course RE not only an intellectually challenging subject but also an intensely relevant one to the current world in which emotional intelligence, the ability to empathise and to understand different points of view, is a vital ingredient of success in a wide range of careers.

Clarification of values

The current time is also a ripe one in which to be helping students to reflect for themselves, to weigh up issues and to consider what is important in life. The world that students are in the process of inheriting is vastly different from that of their teachers' and parents' generation. With an increased emphasis on personal choice and its associated personal accountability, the importance of values to guide students' decisions which affect their own or others' lives has never been greater.

The aims of *Religion in Focus: Christianity in today's world*

To explore fundamental questions which are immediately interesting and relevant to the student.

As teachers we know how difficult it is to motivate and capture the interest of students at KS4. ***Religion in Focus*** aims to start 'where they are at' and to raise issues that young people want to talk about. We have found in our discussions with colleagues in all types of school that the fundamental questions in the new RE syllabuses are just the sort of things that young people want to discuss. This course allows them space to consider these issues – and hopefully to get a GCSE grade out of it too! Each spread starts by raising the issue and asking for an off-the-cuff student response, before leading into teaching about the detailed information and other possible responses to it.

To study selected aspects of a religion in depth rather than attempting a superficial survey.

As teachers we feel strongly that students should have sufficient information, in sufficient detail, in order to study issues from a religious perspective in an informed and mature way. We have therefore attempted to give some detail and a wide variety of sources of authority in dealing with religious teachings about each issue. This course allows students to follow a GCSE RE syllabus in depth. It presents a wide variety of Christian viewpoints, teaching on and responses to fundamental questions of life, and moral issues. It allows students to explore in-depth *why* Christians have a variety of responses to issues. It enables reasoned reflection and clear thinking about issues affecting Christians.

To meet the requirements of the National Criteria The National Criteria for GCSE short course RE describe the aims of RE as follows. The students should:

– *acquire and develop knowledge and develop understanding of the beliefs, values and traditions of one or more religions;*
– *consider the influence of the beliefs, values and traditions associated with one or more religions;*
– *consider religious and other responses to moral issues;*
– *identify, investigate and respond to fundamental questions of life raised by religion and human experience.*

To highlight different viewpoints held by different traditions within a religion.

All GCSE RE syllabuses require students to be able to answer questions from the viewpoint of more than one religion, or more than one perspective within a religion. Even more important than this, we believe that it is vital for young people to be presented with a wide variety of opinions on and responses to issues, so that they can seek guidance in formulating their own responses and support in upholding them.

Teachers preparing students for GCSE may use this book in conjunction with either *Islam in Today's World* or *Judaism in Today's World* to allow a very wide breadth of response in the examination, or they may use just this *Christianity* book and encourage students to seek a variety of Christian opinions in answering questions.

To encourage a personal response from the student but one which is considered and informed by their study of a religion. Facilitating this personal response is the key objective of this series.

Whilst gaining a good grade at GCSE must be a prime aim for all students, there is far more to education than that. The three steps in each investigation – the issue raiser, the in-depth information and the exploration of responses – allow students to engage with the material and encourage them to make their own, reasoned response. Some investigations will be immediately more attractive to each student than others. Yet in order to be 'religiously educated' young people need to study and to be able to formulate, articulate and justify their own views on a wide range of issues; the material that this course provides will encourage that.

Structure of the Student's Book

We have followed the structure of NEAB Syllabus D *Thinking about God and Morality*, while creating resources which suit all syllabuses (see page 8).

Unit 1 introduces concepts dealt with by the rest of the course.

1.1 raises discussion of what moral decisions are and asks students how they make moral decisions.

1.2 explores various sources of authority for Christians as they make decisions.

1.3 and 1.4 provide some basic background to Christianity and to the variety of traditions within the religion, as well as common beliefs.

Units 2–4 deal with moral issues, particularly those required for study in the principal short course syllabuses.

Unit 5 deals with theology.

Unit 1: How do Christians make moral decisions?
1.1   What would you do if . . . ?
1.2   The Moral Ocean
1.3   Christian traditions
1.4   A Christian world view

Unit 2: Issues of life and death
2.1   INTRODUCTION: The sanctity of life
2.2   ABORTION: Why do many Christians oppose abortion?
2.3   EUTHANASIA: Murder, mercy killing or gentle and easy death?
2.4   CAPITAL PUNISHMENT: Does it help to execute murderers?
       Issues of life and death – Review task

Unit 3: Relationships
3.1   INTRODUCTION: The perfect relationship?
3.2   SEX, MARRIAGE AND DIVORCE: Are Christian ideas about marriage out of date?
3.3   HOMOSEXUALITY: Why do Christians disagree about homosexuality?
3.4   PREJUDICE AND DISCRIMINATION 1: How do Christians respond to racism?
3.5   PREJUDICE AND DISCRIMINATION 2: Are women treated as equals in Christianity?
3.6   THE INDIVIDUAL IN SOCIETY: How can Christians serve others?
       Relationships – Review task

Unit 4: Global issues
4.1   INTRODUCTION: How can individuals change the world?
4.2   WEALTH AND POVERTY: How should Christians use their money?
4.3   THE ENVIRONMENT: Responsible stewards or plundering idiots?
4.4   WAR AND PEACE: Is it ever right to fight?
       Global issues – Review task

Unit 5: Arguments about God
5.1   INTRODUCTION: Why do people believe in God?
5.2   ARGUMENTS FOR THE EXISTENCE OF GOD: Can you prove that God exists?
5.3   THE NATURE OF GOD: What is God like?
5.4   HOW GOD MAY BE KNOWN: One God . . . revealed in many ways
5.5   SUFFERING AND EVIL: Why do people suffer?
5.6   LIFE AFTER DEATH: What kind of future do Christians look forward to?
       Arguments about God – Review tasks

Each unit contains a number of in-depth investigations which vary in length according to the complexity of the content. See opposite for the features of each investigation.

Features of an investigation

Investigation title
The title is usually in the form of a question to be investigated. The question itself can be opened up for classroom discussion before you plough into the unit.

Issue raiser
An activity or question, usually based on a case study, a picture or a story introduces the issue and invites an initial response from the student.

Checkpoints
These information boxes provide background information, or explain key words or concepts which students must know for the examination.

Key questions for Christians
These are the religious questions that are most relevant to this issue. These key questions form the basis for the rest of the investigation. They can also be used as class discussion questions in their own right.

Sources
A wide variety of pictures, drawings and real quotations are used in various ways:

- to convey the teaching of various sources of authority
- to highlight divergent opinions within Christianity
- to stimulate students' thinking about an issue
- to humanise the study.

These Sources are the raw material of the course. They are not optional extras. All Sources are used in some way, either in tasks or in questions.

Question panels
These encourage students to read and respond to the text and the Sources. Some are intended for use in class discussion or small group discussion. Some require a brief written answer. Some are ideal for homework. You can select those questions most appropriate to your own plan of work.

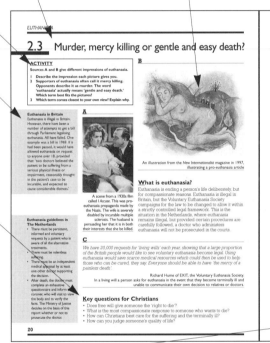

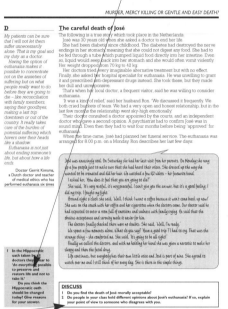

Boxed tasks
These are the main building blocks of the classroom investigation. There are different approaches which allow for differentiation and variety. The purpose of each one is outlined in the detailed teacher's notes. The distinction between the different types of tasks is not rigid but these are the four main categories we have used:

ACTIVITY These may be research-based writing tasks or discussion-style, but they have in common that they require students **to engage creatively or imaginatively** with the material.

DISCUSS These are similar to the questions but are more central to the development of the investigation.

SAVE AS . . . These tasks are designed to help students **to get information into their notebooks** or onto paper for future revision. Often they appear at the end of an activity, allowing the learning that has taken place in the activity to be transferred onto paper.

FOCUS TASK In terms of syllabus coverage and assessment of students' overall grasp of the topics, the Focus Tasks are some of the most important tasks. There is one Focus Task for each key topic in the main syllabuses.

They vary in style from examination-style questions to creative assignments. What they have in common is that they are **summative** tasks which bring together a wide range of learning and insight. They focus on particularly important issues or sum up key ideas from the investigation. Some of them range across a whole unit or bring together ideas from a whole term's work.

Think of them as **the review points** on your journey through the investigation. In the same way as the 'Save As . . .' tasks, they also generate a written response which can be used for revision. There are often worksheets in this Teacher's Resource Book to support the most important tasks, or the 'recording' stages of the tasks.

GCSE syllabuses

This chart summarises the syllabuses at a glance and shows how **Religion in Focus** approaches each family of short course RE syllabuses.

Exam syllabus	London A	MEG B	NEAB D	SEG	WJEC	London B	MEG A	NEAB A
Which *Religion in Focus* books?	*Christianity with Islam and/or Judaism*	*Any one or two, or all three*	*Christianity alone, or with Islam or Judaism*	*Christianity with Islam and/or Judaism*	*Christianity alone, or with Islam and/or Judaism*	*Christianity or Islam or Judaism*	*Christianity or Judaism alone, or any two*	*Christianity or Islam or Judaism*
Topic in book Ways of making moral decisions		✓	✓				✓	
Euthanasia	✓	✓	✓	✓	✓	✓	✓	✓
Abortion	✓	✓	✓	✓			✓	✓
Capital punishment			✓					
Sex	✓	✓	✓	✓	✓		✓	✓
Responsibilities	✓	✓	✓		✓			✓
Prejudice	✓	✓	✓	✓	✓		✓	✓
Wealth & poverty	✓	✓	✓	✓	✓	✓		✓
War & peace		✓	✓	✓		✓	✓	
The environment	✓	✓	✓	✓	✓			
Medical ethics					✓		✓	
Women		✓	✓	✓	✓			✓
Does God exist?	✓	✓	✓	✓				
Why do people suffer?	✓	✓	✓	✓	✓			
What is God like?	✓	✓	✓	✓	✓		✓	
How God may be known	✓	✓	✓	✓	✓			

The first aim of **Religion in Focus** is to cover the core requirements of this first family – those syllabuses focusing on a study of God, morality and ultimate questions. We have structured our material around NEAB Syllabus D, but it is equally suitable for other syllabuses.

Our second aim is to provide innovative teaching strategies which give new life to the teaching of the more traditional core material of syllabuses in this second family, which are based on a systematic study of a given religion.

Planning your course

It is possible to work through the Student's Book as it stands, as a course in its own right. It is also possible to use it flexibly within a course of your own design.

Whichever route you choose, there is clearly a lot more in the book than most schools will need. This is deliberate, to give you flexibility and choice – so planning is essential.

Stage 1: overall course structure

We would suggest that before you plunge into moral issues you tackle the ideas in Unit 1 which establish important general concepts.

We have placed Unit 5 and its study of theology last since we believe that older students who have grappled with moral issues will find the material in Unit 5 more accessible and more rewarding. However, some schools may wish to use Unit 5 first in order to set the scene for the moral issues, showing that how a Christian views God may colour their responses to moral issues.

You will also need to choose from Units 2 to 5 the content needed for your syllabus (see page 8). The book is structured around NEAB Syllabus D but is suited to most other syllabuses.

Stage 2: detailed course planning

For more detailed planning the chart on the next page will help you.

In column 1 note down the investigations you intend to tackle, in the order in which you intend to tackle them.

In column 2 note how long you intend to give to each investigation.

In column 3 select tasks that suit the needs of your class. There are many more tasks and questions than most classes will need. This allows for choice and differentiation, given the very varying time allowed for RE in different schools and given the range of abilities being taught in a typical RE class.

In column 4 note ideas for differentiation. The written material in the Student's Book is suited to average or slightly above average students. The pictorial sources and tasks should be accessible to all students. Some students may need support in dealing with the written material in order to perform the tasks. The teacher's notes and worksheets give a wide variety of support material for all abilities.

In column 5 note additional resources: videos, magazines, IT, etc., which might be needed. As well as commercially produced material, you should ideally already have your own collections of newspaper cuttings, videos of useful TV programmes, tapes of radio programmes, pictures and postcards to stimulate discussion. All of these things can then be added to the resources provided by the course.

Detailed teaching notes

This Teacher's Resource Book provides detailed notes for the use of each investigation in the Student's Book.

The notes explain some of the reasoning behind the course design, and suggest ways of using the tasks as well as other approaches or resources which you could try out.

Photocopiable worksheets

A set of photocopiable worksheets for each unit follows the teaching notes on that unit. The intended use of the worksheets is explained in the notes.

The worksheets serve a wide variety of purposes:

- **Time savers** Some of the more complex grids, tables and sources are reproduced in photocopiable form to reduce the time needed to prepare for an activity; for example: Worksheet 1.6.
- **Support material for the less able** Writing frames, cloze exercises, cut and paste activities are good support for less able students; for example: Worksheet 3.8.
- **Homework** Many of the sheets are suitable for homework, and some of them are specifically designed for it; for example: Worksheet 1.2.
- **Debate and discussion slips** Some sheets provide pre-prepared statements/viewpoints to encourage widespread and balanced discussion; for example: Worksheet 2.10.
- **Games** These are used as a fun way to learn key information or to stimulate thinking; for example: Worksheet 2.4.
- **Word lists**; for example: Worksheet 2.21.
- **Bible reference 'file cards'** These provide at a glance references to useful passages that students should learn to include in their answers; for example: Worksheet 3.19.
- **End of unit tests** These are in the form of a quick quiz to enable students to find out what they have learned and what they need to know; for example: Worksheet 3.20.
- **Examination practice** For each unit there are examination questions which can be used as classroom tasks, homework, examination practice or summary exercises. For example: Worksheet 4.8.
- **'Improve your grade' examination tips** For some of the examination practice sheets you will find answer guidelines of different types, including a real examiner's mark scheme; for example: Worksheet 4.11.

Other planning issues

Some other issues will also affect your general and detailed planning.

Local Agreed Syllabuses

Many Local Agreed Syllabuses simply state that a school is complying with the syllabus for Key Stage 4 if it follows an approved GCSE syllabus in RE or RS. Some, however, have more specific demands and, although we believe that this series will enable teachers to cover the requirements of most Agreed Syllabuses in enabling students to learn both from and about religion, it is not possible for us to be sure we have provided for the distinctive needs of all Local Agreed Syllabuses, so check your syllabus carefully.

GCSE *Short Course RE Planning Sheet*

Syllabus and options followed: _____
Time available: Year 10 _____ Year 11 _____

1: Investigation headings	2: Time to be given	3: Tasks to be used	4: Differentiation techniques to be used	5: Additional resources needed

Christianity in today's world Teacher's Resource Book   © John Murray

Additional resources

Case studies all too quickly go out of date. So we hope that all departments will be actively collecting more recent newspaper cuttings, videos, tapes and pictures to stimulate discussion.

It may be helpful to appoint some students as research assistants who will collect cuttings and other items for the whole group's use, as well as their own. Worksheet 1.5 is a briefing and record sheet for such research.

There are a number of TV series which are worth checking out and taping for use in the classroom. (This is quite legal for classroom use.) Series such as *Heart of the Matter, Everyman, Inside Story*, and *Cutting Edge* are often quite useful. *Panorama* might be helpful for more able students, and *Songs of Praise* (edited of songs) has some very interesting interviews. Both the BBC and Independent Television have also recently brought out new collections of RE material which can be bought or taped. The BBC *RE Collection, Taking Issue*, and *Christianity in Today's World* are worth looking at.

Charities and Christian organisations are another good source of information. These provide information about their own work and may also sell videos and other resources; many have education departments. Teachers must remember that these are charities and may expect a donation, also that they are more likely to be helpful if one student writes on behalf of the whole group rather than all sending begging letters. Some of the material will also be biased to the viewpoint of the charity, naturally, and so care should be taken when using it.

A list of useful addresses of denominations and organisations is provided on pages 13–14. This could be given to students, but its primary use is to help the teacher in locating additional resources from the original sources. Details of addresses of various organisations (and also statistics) can be obtained from the annually published *UK Christian Handbook*. This is an expensive tome but useful. It might possibly be bought by an LEA adviser or group of schools and held centrally as a resource.

Information technology

IT is increasingly valuable in RE. It has had a slow start but there is now some useful software for RE, and not all specifically from RE publishers.

IT can add variety to teaching styles, but there are drawbacks. There is the danger of students taking too long over work and 'experimenting' with the technology rather than really working at RE. Teachers must also guard against the temptation for students to plagiarise material from electronic sources and pass it off as their own work. However, these problems can be eradicated with careful planning and supervision.

There is an obvious place in RE for using commercially available software or the Internet to widen your resource base in research, particularly for reference material. CD-Roms exist such as *Aspects of Religion* (Nelson), and Lion Publishing has a range of useful, specifically

Christian, material. The *Guardian* CD-Rom is a useful tool for researching issues from newspapers, and electronic encyclopaedias are helpful in finding definitions and legal material. Lat Blaylock at CEM (see address list) has compiled a useful list of addresses on the World Wide Web, and CEM also has a publication about IT and RE.

Wordprocessing and desktop publishing can of course improve the presentation of students' work (for example, Worksheet 3.7). Sunrise Software and Churchill Publishing have an excellent selection of Clipart. Students can be helped to identify what illustration is appropriate for the context.

Wordprocessing can also help in students' conceptual grasp of issues. The work undertaken by the NCET-sponsored project on IT in History, regarding the role of wordprocessing in helping develop students' thinking skills and organisational skills, is well worth looking at for cross-curricular implications.

The examination

Many of the tasks in the Student's Book are designed to enable students to record information in some form. How this is done – books or folders, or whatever – is left to the teacher to decide. This is the students' written record to return to when they come to revise for the examination. By writing down or recording information in some way students should be internalising it more thoroughly and thus learning more.

However, the need to record in a revisable form is sometimes at odds with making an activity interesting and engaging. So on occasions we have given students more help by bringing out the main learning points they will need to remember. The 'Save As . . .' tasks have already been mentioned, as has the role of Focus Tasks in creating a revisable record.

This Resource Book has end of unit tests for each of Units 2–5. These are designed to ease students' recall of content they will need for the exam.

We have included exam-style questions as review tasks at the end of each unit in the Student's Book, and examination practice worksheets in this Resource Book. Ensure you also use questions from your own examination if we have not included examples from that syllabus.

As the new syllabuses mature, Chief Examiners and Examination Boards will develop their question papers in the light of responses each year from candidates and their teachers. Examination Boards always find such responses after the exam useful. The teaching unions have response forms which may be sent, or a simple letter will suffice.

Coursework

It is possible to tackle GCSE short course RE without doing coursework, but there are some syllabuses which offer it as an option. Many tasks in the Student's Book can be adapted as coursework tasks. Students should be encouraged to use, but not to plagiarise, the book as a source for their coursework. The teacher's notes in this Resource Book give advice about additional sources of information.

Supporting non-specialist teachers

In the majority of schools RE is taught by a combination of specialists and non-specialists, and it is important that the specialists offer the non-specialists support. We have attempted to provide material to stimulate the students and the teachers alike but you will need to monitor carefully the effectiveness of the tasks you have chosen, and to compare classroom experiences with other teachers. It is vital to plan well for lessons by reading material in advance and gathering any extra resources such as videos or newspapers and other source materials.

Using the faith community

As we have already emphasised Christianity is about real life. It is a religion, and a way of life, that is followed by real people, in the real world. This dynamic nature is not something that is easy to capture in a textbook. We would urge you therefore to make the most of the faith communities of Christians around your school.

It may be that Christian teachers might be willing to talk about their own faith in relation to specific issues. The local churches may be interested in coming into school to talk about their beliefs and stances. Panels of local Christians could respond to students' questions about topics they are studying. Students might go out to see Christian action at work.

Using real people from faith communities presents many opportunities but also a few pitfalls to be avoided. So here are some guidelines to help you make the most of your faith communities.

Ways of using visitors from faith communities in RE lessons
- Interview the visitors.
- Set up a panel with visitors from different denominations or traditions to respond to questions or debate issues. This could aim to highlight denominational differences, or similarities.
- Invite visitors to discuss with students one-to-one or one-to-two.
- Invite visitors to give talks about specific issues.
- Invite visitors to describe their sources of authority on a moral issue.
- Invite visitors to lead a workshop or seminar on a specific issue.
- Invite them to work with a small group of more, or less, able students.

Guidelines on using members of faith communities
- Always talk to visitors first and ensure that they are suited to working with students. Can they speak at the right level?
- Ensure that visitors understand why they are involved. For example, ensure that they know they are not there to convert students.
- Prepare your students. Advise them about appropriate behaviour, responses and courtesy.
- Prepare your resources and questions etc. well in advance of the lesson.
- Be hospitable. Arrange for students to meet visitors and provide hospitality if possible. Check dietary requirements in advance.
- Ensure that visitors know a bit about your course and syllabus, what you have covered and are about to cover, and their place in it.
- Confirm all arrangements in writing.
- Be sensitive to the visitor – might they have difficulties if confronted with others of different views (including the students)?
- Express your gratitude. Get students to write to thank the visitors. One of our schools ran a competition for students to produce their own 'thankyou' cards to be used to write to thank RE visitors.

Using your students as a resource

Some of the Sources in the Student's Book may raise controversy. Faced by a Source expressing the view of a certain tradition some students may protest, 'I'm a Christian (Catholic, Methodist, etc.) and I don't believe that.' It will be a timely reminder that the students in your class are your richest teaching resource when they are part of the very faith community you are investigating and could greatly enhance class discussion. At the very least it will help demonstrate the diversity of Christian traditions (see the Checkpoint on page 6 of the Student's Book).

This opportunity has a caveat attached. Care will need to be taken throughout the course so that students who are members of faith communities are not offended either by attitudes with which they could never agree, or by comments made by other students.

Likewise some of the moral issues or decisions may be very close to home for some students, so be sensitive to their feelings.

Addresses

Organisations and charities

These are arranged by the unit for which they will be most relevant although a few cross the unit boundaries.

Unit 2: Issues of life and death

Cruse Bereavement Care
Cruse House, 126 Sheen Road
Richmond, Surrey TW9 1UR
0181 940 4818

EXIT (Voluntary Euthanasia Society)
13 Prince of Wales Terrace
London W8 3PG
0171 937 7770

LIFE (anti-abortion campaigners)
1a Newbold Terrace
Leamington Spa CV32 4EA
01926 421587

Prison Fellowship (Christian concern for prisoners and their families)
PO Box 945
Chelmsford, Essex CM2 7PX
01245 490249

Society for the Protection of the Unborn Child
7 Tufton Street
London SW1P 3QN
0171 222 5845

Unit 3: Relationships

Broken Rites (Anglican group concerned with breakdown of clergy marriages)
30 Steavenson Street
Bowburn, Durham DH6 5BA
0191 377 0205

Catholic Marriage Advisory Council
Clitheroe House, 1 Blythe Mews, Blythe Road
London W14 0MW
0181 371 1341

Commission for Racial Equality
10/12 Allington House
London SW1E 5EH

Corrymeela (community drawing Protestants and Roman Catholics together in N. Ireland)
8 Upper Crescent
Belfast BT7 1NT
01232 325008

L'Arche (communities for the mentally handicapped)
The Anchorage, 25 Fairfield Crescent
Liverpool 6
0151 260 0422

Lesbian and Gay Christian Movement
Oxford House, Derbyshire Street
London E2 6HG
0171 739 1249

Lighthouse Family Trust (Christian support for families)
72 Longacre
Chelmsford, Essex CM1 3BJ
01245 494838

Unit 4: Global issues

Animal Aid
7 Castle Street
Tonbridge, Kent TN9 1BH

Animal Christian Concern
46 St Margaret's Road
Horsforth, Leeds LS18 5BG
0113 258 3517

CAFOD (Catholic Agency for Overseas Development)
Romero Close, Stockwell Road
London SW9 9TY
0171 733 7900

Christian Aid (overseas aid and development work)
PO Box 100
London SE1 7RT
0171 620 4444

CND (Campaign for Nuclear Disarmament)
22/24 Underwood Street
London N1 7JY

Christian CND
St Mary's Church, Bramall Lane
Sheffield S2 4QZ
0114 273 9047

Friends of the Earth
26–28 Underwood Street
London N1 7JQ
0171 490 1555

Greenpeace
Canonbury Villas
London N1 2PN
0171 354 5100

Nicaraguan Solidarity Campaign
23 Beverden Street
London N1 6BH

Pax Christi (Christian pacifists, largely Catholic)
9 Henry Road
London N4 2LH
0181 800 4612

Society of St Vincent de Paul (Roman Catholic,
alleviating poverty)
546 Sauchiehall Street
Glasgow G2 3NG
0141 332 7752

TEAR Fund (The Evangelical Alliance Relief Fund)
11 Station Road
Teddington, Middlesex TW11 9AA
0181 977 9144

World Vision (development and aid)
599 Avebury Boulevard
Milton Keynes, Bucks MK9 3PG
01908 841000

World Wide Fund for Nature
Education Dept.
Weyside Park
Godalming, Surrey GU7 1XR

Christian denominations and agencies

Baptist Union
Baptist House, PO Box 44, 129 Broadway
Didcot, Oxfordshire OX11 8RT
01235 512077

Catholic Education Service
38/40 Eccleston Square
London SW1P 1LT

CARE (Christian Action Research and Education)
53 Romney Street
London SW1P 3RF
0171 233 0455

Christian Education Movement
Royal Buildings, Victoria Street
Derby DE1 1GW
01332 296655

Christians in Science
Atholl Centre, Atholl Road
Pitlochry, Perthshire PH16 5BX
01796 473044

The Church of England
Church House, Westminster
London SW1P 3NZ

Council of Christians and Jews
1 Dennington Park Road
London NW6 1AX
0171 794 8178

Intercessors for Britain (prayer fellowship)
14 Orchard Road, Moreton
Wirral, Merseyside L46 8TS
0151 677 6767

The Julian Meetings (contemplative prayer)
32 Grosvenor Road
Norwich NR2 2PZ
01603 666455

Methodist Church
25 Marylebone Road
London NW1 5JR
0171 486 5502

National Society (Church of England society for
promoting RE)
Church House, Westminster
London SW1P 3NZ
0171 222 1672

Orthodox Church Information Service
64 Prebend Gardens
London W6 0XY

Orthodox Church (Southern district)
10 Heathwood Gardens, Charlton
London SE7 8EP
0181 854 3090

The Religious Society of Friends (Quakers)
Friends House, Euston Road
London NW1 2BJ

Salvation Army
101 Queen Victoria Street
London EC4 4EP
0171 236 5222

UNIT I

How do Christians make moral decisions?

Overview

This introductory unit establishes some basic ideas:

- the nature of morality (1.1)
- sources of moral authority (1.2)
- what we mean by Christian traditions (1.3)
- the link between religious beliefs and values and behaviour. (1.4)

Starting strategies

Page 1

Students should already have followed a comprehensive Local Agreed Syllabus for RE at Key Stage 3, which will have given them an understanding of the basic beliefs and practices of Christianity. This cartoon is to get students talking about their attitude to what they already know. **Worksheet 1.1** reproduces the cartoon. The completed worksheets can be stored and re-used at the end of the course, when students can discuss how their views have changed (if at all).

1.1 What would you do if...?

A single spread introduces the idea of moral decisions.

It may be useful to show a video clip before or after using the four dilemmas. A useful one is from the BBC series *Taking Issue*, Programme 3: *Wealth and Poverty*, which includes a short drama about three young boys who live in a squat and are hungry. They see a baker's shop full of tempting cakes and they think about stealing from it at night. It is useful to show the first part of the drama and stop it (before they actually do break in) and ask students whether they think the boys should break in or not. Discuss what the moral issues at stake are. Show the rest of the drama and discuss it further. There are deeper moral issues here: is it right that the boys were in this situation to start with? Whose fault is it?

Page 3

SAVE AS ... Worksheet 1.2 supports this task. It provides a template for a moral dilemma diary, ideal for homework over a weekend.

An alternative strategy, if students find it difficult to identify their own moral decisions, would be to focus on a current TV soap opera. Students could watch an episode (or a whole week's) and note all the moral dilemmas that arise for a chosen favourite character.

1.2 The moral ocean

This investigation explores sources of moral authority. For some students these may be quite different to those that Christians will resort to, or there may be some overlap.

Page 4

ACTIVITY Worksheet 1.3 is a copy of the Moral Ocean illustration for the students' use. It can be re-used later in connection with a specific moral decision, for example in investigation 2.3.

It is worth discussing early on how Christians use the Bible in making moral decisions. Because some GCSE syllabuses make a feature of knowing Bible references to support Christian viewpoints, it is easy for students to slip into a mistaken assumption that Christians rely on such text as gobbets of random wisdom. Clearly this is not the case. The Bible is a varied and complex book which is capable of some widely differing interpretations (see Worksheet 3.9 for an illustration of this) but there is also a coherent story running through it of God's relationship with people, which establishes important principles. It is these principles that guide Christians, rather than 'proof texts'.

Furthermore, the Bible engages most with the biggest concerns of its time. Some of the moral issues dealt with in GCSE RE were also important issues in biblical times, others less so. You could ask students to read the Contents list of the Student's book. Which issues would students expect to have been important in biblical times, and which not?

In fact the majority of the GCSE RE moral issues are addressed head-on by the Bible even if they have different weight from today and even if the biblical context and solutions are sometimes different from those of the present day. We'd say that all these topics are addressed directly by the Bible: marriage, sex, adultery, homosexuality, racism, relationship between rich and poor, war and peace, different roles of men and women, the individual in society, capital punishment, the environment. Two topics are addressed only indirectly in the Bible, through the sanctity of life: abortion and euthanasia.

However, the point remains that whether the Bible addresses issues directly or indirectly it is the *principles* that guide Christians today, not just the practices or the precedents and certainly not the 'Bible references'.

Page 4

SAVE AS ... Worksheet 1.4 provides a sheet to note examples of people who have taken absolutist or relativist stances on issues. Students will need to be reminded through the course to look out for such examples to note.

Students could also gather their own collection of newspaper cuttings which give examples of moral dilemmas. **Worksheet 1.5** suggests a mechanism for doing this.

1.3 Christian traditions

This investigation introduces students to the broad traditions and denominations of this country. In this book we are mainly using examples from the Catholic tradition and from the Protestant tradition (usually although not exclusively the Church of England).

Page 6

ACTIVITY Worksheet 1.6 is a simplified version of the illustration in Source A to support the Activity.

For the Activity it is advisable to stick to the main traditions and denominations and avoid the inclusion of sects such as the Jehovah's Witnesses, since their relationship to the mainstream denominations is both confusing and controversial. They would not be deemed by the examiners to be appropriate examples of a Christian tradition to use in the examination.

It may be useful for teachers to make a simplified tracing (trunk only) of the illustration onto OHT, then over the course add on branches using overlays, showing where any speakers or visitors who come into school fit into the 'vine'.

CHECKPOINT It is very important that students note and understand the point of this, that Christians do not fit neatly into these categories. Looking closely at a single church is a little like looking closely at a single class. Students may all be sitting in the same room, reading the same book, hearing the same teacher, but that does not mean they think the same way as the person to their right or left, nor that when school is ended today they will go off and watch the same TV programme or listen to the same music as the person in front!

1.4 A Christian world view

Since this course will be building on a study of Christianity lower down the school, this treatment is deliberately skeletal. However, each of these beliefs is investigated in greater depth in Unit 5 if you need clarification.

If you need further help, two BBC videos may also be of use in this area: *Belief File, Christianity*, Programme 1: *What's it all about?* is useful for introducing less able students to the basics of the faith; while *Christianity in Today's World*, Programme 1: *Christianity in a Changing World* is a fast-moving introduction for all.

Page 9

FOCUS TASK You may wish to write out and copy simplified statements for the students beforehand. For example (anti-clockwise from the top left):

- God made the Earth. God made people.
- In the beginning the Earth was perfect. People have spoiled it.
- People have free will. Many reject God.
- Jesus shows the way God wants people to live.
- Each person is special to God.
- People need to work with others.
- God is in control.

Page 10

A moral code

SOURCE E The Golden Rule is so widely accepted that maybe it doesn't get the analysis and attention it deserves. You could discuss everyday examples of where it is observed and where it is not. You could ask students to create a short scene in which people either follow or ignore the Golden Rule. Then discuss its usefulness and shortcomings as a moral base.

ACTIVITY A Worksheet 1.7 is a survey sheet to run this Ten Commandments survey task. This can lead into a class discussion along these lines:

> 'Christians follow two moral codes: the Ten Commandments given to Moses in the Old Testament; and the law of the love taught by Jesus in the New Testament. Which do you think is better: to keep laws or to love others?'

Alternatively, students could create Highway Code style moral 'road signs'. They could swap signs and see if they can interpret others' signs. This can lead into a discussion: 'We obviously do not have signs like this. Why not? What do we have instead?'. This in turn will lead easily into the class debate suggested by **Activity B**.

Worksheet 1.8 is the first of a series of examination practice questions which picks up on ideas introduced throughout Unit 1. It could be used now or later. If used now answers might be shallow. If used later the students would have abundant examples to use. For example, the issue of abortion is ideal for examining the distinction between something that is legal and something that is deemed morally acceptable by all Christians.

How do you react to religion?

1 Colour in the cartoon character that is nearest to your feeling about religion at this stage in your life.

2 Write about why you chose that character.

_____

_____

_____

3 List up to three occasions in your life when you have come into contact with religion (or it has come into contact with you!)

_____

_____

_____

_____

4 Try to explain to yourself how you feel/felt about each of those experiences, and why.

5 If someone asked you whether you were a religious person, what would you say? Try to focus your thoughts and write your answer in this small box. Give a reason, not just yes or no.

Keep this worksheet – you may want to refer back to it later in the course.

A moral dilemma diary

1 Use this chart to record every time you have to make a decision between right and wrong.

Name _____

Situation (include time, place)	Possible actions (explain what you could have done in that situation)	What I did and why	Outcome(s) (explain what happened as a result)

2 Now complete these sentences to explain what you have learned from the exercise.

a) *About myself* I have learned that _____

_____

b) *About making moral decisions* I have learned that _____

_____

The Christian Moral Ocean

Making moral decisions is a bit like steering a ship through dangerous or exciting unknown waters. To help you reach a decision you are happy about and which you feel is right, there are 'islands' you can visit. These islands are your 'sources of moral authority'. What route would you take? What route would a Christian take?

Islands labelled: Teachers, Past experience, Secular wisdom, Conscience, Just 17, The Pope, DECISION I'VE MADE, WHAT SHALL I DO?, Parents, TV, Jesus, Satan, Local priest or minister, The Bible.

1 You can call at five islands before you make your final decision. Mark your route. If we have missed off some of your favoured sources of moral authority, you can label other islands.

2 What differences, if any, might there be between your route and the route of a Christian?

3 What do the choices you have made say about you?

WORKSHEET 1.4

Absolute and relative morality

ABSOLUTE MORALITY – this is when a person believes that there is a right course of action in a moral dilemma that is true in all situations, regardless of culture, religious tradition, time or age. For example: 'it is always wrong to kill'.

RELATIVE MORALITY – this is when a person has strong beliefs or principles but they believe that different courses of action might be needed in different situations. For example: 'it is usually wrong to kill, but sometimes it might be necessary for a particular reason'.

In your exam you may need to give examples of people who have absolutist or relativist views on various moral issues. As you work through the course, note down on this sheet examples of each. Make sure that you note clearly where you found these examples so that you can refer back to them.

One example from your book is given to start you off. But don't limit yourself to what is in the book. Include examples you have seen on television or read elsewhere. You will probably need to continue on a separate sheet.

You will not be able to get an example of both absolute and relative morality for every issue. You will also find that you have many more entries in one column than the other. You will be able to discuss in class why that is.

Issue	An absolutist example (include reference to source)	A relativist example (include reference to source)
Abortion	'Abortion has been considered to be murder since the first centuries of the Church and nothing permits it to be considered otherwise'. Pope Paul VI speaking in 1970 (page 17 of Student's Book)	'Are we sure that it is always the just and loving thing to bring into this demanding, complex world a badly deformed . . . individual?' L. Kalland (page 18 of Student's Book)

Christianity in today's world Teacher's Resource Book

© John Murray

Morality in the news

It would be very useful to build up a collection of newspaper or magazine reports about the issues that you will cover. Keep an eye open for articles which shed further light on people's attitudes towards the moral issues you are studying, or their beliefs about God. You can use these for class work, homework, coursework, or revision.

Read through the Contents page of the Student's Book so that you are aware of the content of the course, or ask your teacher for a copy of the examination syllabus that you are studying.

You could appoint a research assistant – parents and grandparents are good at cutting things out of papers for you!

Keep your cuttings safe (e.g. in plastic wallets) and number them. Use this chart as a reference or index to your cuttings.

Article number	Topic (i.e. which investigations in the book is it relevant to?)	Brief summary (less than ten words if possible)	Source (i.e. where you found it – in what paper, on what date)

The Christian family tree

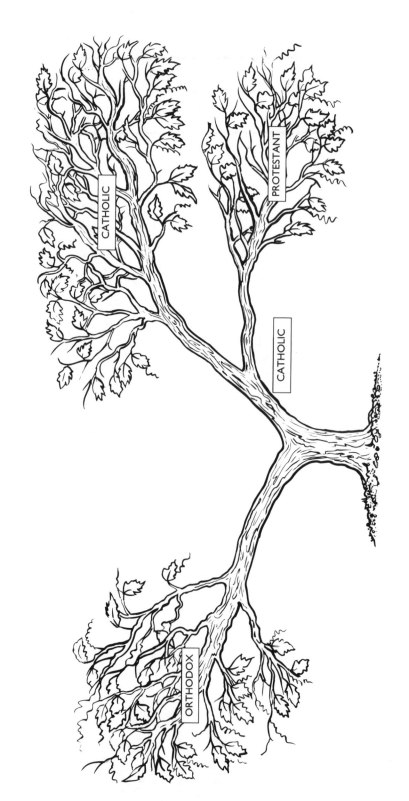

CATHOLIC

PROTESTANT

CATHOLIC

ORTHODOX

1 On a small slip of paper write a description of any other Christian tradition or Church that you know about.
2 Place your description where you think it belongs on this tree.
3 Check your placing with your teacher, then stick it down.
4 As you meet visitors from the Christian Faith Community, add their names to the tree in the appropriate place.

Christianity in today's world Teacher's Resource Book © John Murray

Your Top Ten Commandments

Many people claim to follow the Ten Commandments as a moral code. Here is a list of commandments: the original ten plus some others.

I Tick the ten that you think are most important to include in a moral code today.

Commandment	Tick	Your comments on why this commandment is important
Worship God		
Do not make false gods or worship idols		
Do not misuse God's name		
Keep the Sabbath day holy		
Respect your father and mother		
Do not murder		
Do not commit adultery		
Do not steal		
Do not falsely accuse anyone		
Do not desire something that belongs to someone else		
Don't drink and drive		
Treat others as you'd like to be treated yourself		
Don't be violent		
Don't be racist		
Care for the environment		
Don't take illegal drugs		
Be loyal to your friends		
Don't be sexist		
Always tell the truth		
Don't have sex before marriage		

2 Compile a class Top Ten and compare it with Source F on page 10 of your book.

3 Now complete this sentence to summarise what the result tells you about your class's moral code:

Our results show me that _____

_____

_____

_____

WORKSHEET 1.8

Examination practice: Morality

Speaker A

Speaker B

a) What is 'morality'? (1)

_____

b) Explain the difference between 'absolute' morality and 'relative' morality. (2)

_____

_____

_____

c) Name **three** sources of authority for members of **one** religious tradition you have studied. (3)

   i) _____

   ii) _____

   iii) _____

d) Is there any difference between an action being 'wrong' and it being 'against your religion'? Give an example to support your viewpoint. (3)

_____

_____

_____

_____

e) As Speaker B implies, sometimes the values held by society in general may conflict with a person's religious beliefs. Give **one** example of an action which is not against the law but which some religious people might consider to be 'wrong'. (2)

_____

_____

f) Do the religious beliefs people hold affect their behaviour? Give examples to support your opinion. (3)

_____

_____

_____

_____

NEAB (GCSE short course) RE Syllabus D, Specimen Paper 2

    Christianity in today's world Teacher's Resource Book   © John Murray

UNIT 2
Issues of life and death

Overview

The introductory investigation (2.1) focuses on *the* key idea for this unit – the **sanctity of life**. Then separate investigations look at abortion (2.2), euthanasia (2.3) and capital punishment (2.4).

At the time of writing, the NEAB Syllabus D has Euthanasia as a compulsory area of study although the compulsory areas may rotate in future.

The unit also investigates the concepts of quality of life and justice, which are going to be useful in later units. It is important that students are familiar with, and able to use freely, these and other key terms cited by your chosen syllabus.

Note that for each of Units 2–5 there is a **word list** worksheet, which you may want to give out to students at the start of the course. They are Worksheets 2.21, 3.21, 4.15 and 5.19.

Starting strategies

Page 11
Today human beings have greater power over life and death than ever before, especially through the advances that have been made in medical technology. Is this good or bad? The cartoon is designed to provoke discussion of this question. **Worksheet 2.1** uses this cartoon. It could be used again at the end of the unit to re-evaluate the students' initial responses.

Other possible starting strategies:

- a brainstorm of words that students associate with the word 'life' and with 'death'
- a 'stilling' exercise: the teacher asks students to focus on their feelings about life and death, leading to the drawing of a poster
- students could scour newspapers and magazines for articles and pictures about life and death (e.g. abortion, poverty and starvation, birth and death announcements, obituaries summing up people's lives...)
- a number of the videos mentioned in the detailed notes below could also be used to introduce the topic.

2.1 The sanctity of life

This three-page investigation introduces the key idea for the unit – the Christian belief in the sanctity of life – through a study of the controversy over frozen embryos.

Page 13
ACTIVITY Students might be guided to different roles for the phone-in: a doctor called to thaw out the embryos, couples who have discovered too late that their embryo has been thawed out, childless couples who would

willingly provide 'foster wombs' and adopt, and church leaders called on to make comment.

Alternatively, the same roles could be taken in a small group role play. All those playing doctors etc. should first get together and agree their arguments, the groups should then mix up with one 'expert' in each new group to argue through the issue.

Worksheet 2.2 provides extension material about four Churches' views on embryology, for students to use for the second point of their articles in Activity 2.

Page 14
FOCUS TASK Worksheet 2.3 provides support for this task. The 'cells' and Bible references can be cut out, matched up, then used as the basis for the poster.

The BBC video *Words into Action, Life and Death* has Psalm 139, acted out with feeling. It might be helpful to play this to students and ask for their response: does the belief that God 'knows' the unborn fetus give it protection?

A lot of the dilemmas in this unit are relevant to doctors. **Worksheet 2.4** can be used at any point through the unit. It is a game called 'Doctor's Dilemma' which explores the different issues raised in this unit through a doctor's eyes. It is played in groups of four.

In the game you will find we have chosen how to award points for each decision – which is making a moral judgement in itself! A worthwhile extension of this game will be to discuss in class how far students agree with our scores for each decision.

2.2 Why do many Christians oppose abortion?

The phrasing of the key question may seem to have prejudged the central issue – after all Christians do have different views on the topic, as is clear from the evidence in the investigation. However, Christians are prominent in the anti-abortion movement and we have therefore taken as our key question why that should be so.

Abortion is an emotive subject. Some students in the group may have had experience of it themselves or through friends or family. So whilst it is important to explore various viewpoints, it is also important to treat this (as all issues) with sensitivity.

Students can be satisfactorily prepared for some examination questions if they simply know arguments for and against abortion, some Bible teaching and Church teaching, but we have gone into greater depth than this. One reason for this is that abortion is a good topic through which to investigate absolute and relative morality, because while certain traditions have authoritative teaching laying out an absolutist position on abortion – notably the Roman Catholic Church – in practice individual Christians in all traditions including the Catholic tradition find it quite difficult to take such an absolutist stance and are instinctively more relativist. They feel there are a lot of situational factors to be taken into account in making a decision.

Page 15

ACTIVITY Worksheet 2.5 supports the first Activity and also relates the discussion of absolute and relative morality to the students' own beliefs.

Note that we return to Sammi for Activity B on page 19.

CHECKPOINT The text deliberately does not spell out how abortions are carried out. Some students will ask and the teacher needs to respond appropriately. Broadly, there are three main methods of ending a pregnancy.

1   The first is not termed abortion. In this case a pill (the so-called 'morning after pill') is taken which prevents any zygote from embedding in the lining of the womb.
2   Up to about twelve weeks of pregnancy *dilation* and *curettage* is used to suck the fetus from the womb through a tube inserted through the vagina. Larger pieces of tissue are crushed and pulled out with forceps and the womb cleared of any remaining material. This is done usually under general anaesthetic.
3   In later abortions (rarer and mainly in the case of disability) the fetus is first injected with drugs to end life and then labour is induced and the dead fetus is delivered in the normal way.

Page 16

When does life begin?

ACTIVITY Worksheet 2.6 supports this task with a copy of Source B and the questions.

Page 17

What does Christianity teach about abortion?

Question 7 This refers to **Worksheet 1.4**, which has already been started off for the students.

Pages 18–19

Christian views on abortion

SOURCE K This mentions 'quality of life' as a determinant. We have not gone into detail here, since we have investigated it in more detail on page 25 as part of the euthanasia investigation. However, it is worth noting that some Christians who otherwise oppose abortion sometimes would allow abortion if the child would have little quality of life, for example if it might be dreadfully handicapped and might require constant medical care or frequent operations; or if it might be so brain-damaged that it would not be able to relate to others and might never achieve independence. Others would not be swayed at all by the quality of life argument and clearly quality of life is not an objective measure. Students could discuss what factors would influence the 'quality of life' expectations of an unborn child.

ACTIVITY A This could work well as a physical activity. Mark a line on the floor of the class with string and labels, or on the board. Have the Source letter on a large sheet and students should discuss where on the class line to place it. They could appoint someone to summarise the Source.

Students will want to express their own views. Ask students to stand on the appropriate place on the line for them. This could lead to a general discussion of their views and the views in the Sources. It may be that your students take strong stances on either side. They should be encouraged to explain their views very carefully.

The Activity could equally well work as a cut-and-paste activity.

Other resources: It may be possible to supplement pages 18–19 with a debate including outside speakers and/or using material from agencies who are pro-life or pro-choice. If so, the origin of the source and its bias must be stressed to students. Many agencies are willing to come into school to talk, but again their bias must be noted, and the aims of the course as an RE syllabus must be borne in mind.

Page 19

FOCUS TASK This requires the students to write a demanding essay. **Worksheet 2.7** supports the essay-writing process. All students will benefit from such guidance in the early stages of a GCSE course. Many will still need it at the end. This worksheet also provides a model for later extended-writing tasks. Different styles of 'writing frame' can be found on other worksheets, for example 2.17, 3.14, 5.2, 5.6.

Worksheet 2.8 provides exam-style questions reviewing work on abortion.

2.3 Murder, mercy killing, or gentle and easy death?

The first spread focuses on a moving story of euthanasia in Holland; the second spread looks at Christian attitudes towards euthanasia; the third spread looks at hospices and the concept of 'quality of life'.

In the BBC *RE Collection*, the programme on *Life and Death* is an excellent introductory video to use for the topic of euthanasia.

Page 20

What is euthanasia?

To avoid confusion make sure students have got their definitions clear.

Passive euthanasia (which means not doing anything to prevent death or prolong life) is not legally euthanasia and students would be well advised not to use the term euthanasia to describe it. Many Christians would allow for passive euthanasia. Likewise turning off a life-support system is not termed euthanasia and in exams students should not describe it as such.

For this moral issue therefore we are really concerned

with **active euthanasia** (i.e. taking deliberate action to speed death, for example giving a patient an injection to put them to sleep).

Voluntary euthanasia is active euthanasia at the request of the patient him/herself.

The investigation focuses on voluntary euthanasia since this is the area of greatest debate. Voluntary euthanasia is illegal in Britain. A doctor or relative who helps someone to die can be charged with murder. However, some people in Britain are seeking to change the law, especially EXIT (The Voluntary Euthanasia Society).

The issue is not clear-cut for Christians. Some would argue that voluntary euthanasia could be morally right and that everyone has the right to die in dignity when and how they request. They would look for quality of life as the test. Others would argue that life should always be preserved and that euthanasia is really murder, and any concession to voluntary euthanasia is a very dangerous path to tread.

The issue of suffering complicates the issue, and Christians are not agreed about the role of suffering. Some would argue that a God of love would not want human beings to suffer. Others would point out how some good can come through suffering. We return to the topic of suffering in investigation 5.5.

Page 22

Christian principles

SOURCE E Worksheet 2.9 provides an alternative approach to that of question 1. It gets students to balance the scales for themselves.
Question 4 This asks which of Sources G–I are examples of absolute/relative morality. In our view the answer is G = relative; H, I = absolute.

On page 4 of Unit 1, it was suggested that students note examples of absolute and relative morality as they go through the book. You could remind them to record these examples (on Worksheet 1.4).
Question 5 Note that Quakers believe that Christians must personally work out what is right with God in every situation. They believe that God will always know the right course of action, when we as humans may not. By listening to God and to others (including the teaching of other religions), the individual believer can arrive at a Godly solution. You could chart a Quaker's progress through the Moral Ocean (Worksheet 1.3).

Page 23

Should voluntary euthanasia be allowed in Britain?

FOCUS TASK A You could save this debate till you reach page 25 when students will have investigated the hospice option and the quality of life argument. You will have a more informed debate if you use it at that stage. For task 2, students should list *all* their reasons in part a) and choose their most important one in part b).

How you set up the debate will depend on what

spread of views you have in the classroom. We expect most GCSE groups to be pro-euthanasia and so that side of the debate may need less priming – thus the bias in our statements on page 23, which fall six against euthanasia, two for.

Worksheet 2.10 gives more statements, balanced eight for and eight against. The statements from page 23 are summarised, and some others are added, culled from the rest of the investigation and elsewhere. Hand them out to guarantee a good spread of views.

FOCUS TASK B For this essay you could refer the students back to **Worksheet 2.7** which guided them through the essay-writing process. In this case their research phase should gather:

a) Definitions: what euthanasia is and what is the law.
b) Why Christians might agree with the statement, including the biblical basis.
c) Why Christians might disagree, including the biblical basis.
d) What the student's own view is.

This essay may also be best tackled after studying page 25.

Page 24

The hospice movement

The hospice movement deserves more space than we have given it here since it is a central part of the Christian response to the problem of terminal illness. **Worksheet 2.11** is an extension or homework sheet about the work of a Christian hospice nurse.

The BBC *Words into Action* programme on *Life and Death* includes a case study of Helen House, a hospice for children in Oxford.

Page 25

What is quality of life?

FOCUS TASK You could support some students by giving them some 'quality of life' statements to choose from: Quality of life is . . . loads of CDs; knowing God; a good relationship; a nice house; a good job; a happy family; a sense of fulfilment; being active; doing what you want; . . . . Students can then place these in order of importance for themselves and add any that they think are missing.

Worksheet 2.12 is another angle on the absolute/relative debate. Is it possible to be against abortion but pro-euthanasia? Or vice versa? Are they really similar issues?

Worksheet 2.13 provides examination practice on euthanasia. The continuation sheet suggests a model answer which students can discuss.

2.4 Does it help to execute murderers?

Whereas abortion and euthanasia are easily personalised, with the distance we now have from capital punishment it is easy for debates about it to become blasé and to slip into generalisations which ignore the people involved and the issues of life and death that affect them. We have tried to avoid this by focusing on individuals. The first spread looks at the punishment background, which is required by the syllabuses; the second is based on interviews with three women serving life imprisonment for murder; the third spread focuses on Myra Hindley and John Spenkelink.

You could open up this whole debate with a jolt by reading to students two contrasting but real accounts of capital punishment in action; possibly a contemporary one, e.g. Source F from page 31 about the death of John Spenkelink in the USA; and a historical one, e.g. this letter from Lord Byron to his publisher John Murray in May 1817:

The day before I left Rome I saw three robbers guillotined – the ceremony – including the masked priests – the half-naked executioners – the bandaged criminals – the black Christ and his banner – the scaffold – the soldiery – the slow procession – and the quick rattle and heavy fall of the axe – the splash of the blood – and the ghastliness of the exposed heads – was altogether more impressive than the vulgar and ungentlemanly dirty 'new drop' and dog-like agony of the infliction upon the sufferers of the English sentence [hanging]. Two of these men behaved calmly enough – but the first of the three died with great terror and reluctance – which was very horrible – he would not lie down – then his neck was too large for the aperture – and the priest was obliged to drown his exclamations by still louder exhortations – the head was off before the eye could trace the blow – the first head was cut off close to the ears – the other two were taken off more cleanly. The pain seems little and yet the effect to the spectator – and the preparation for the criminal – is very striking and chilling. The first turned me quite hot and thirsty – and made me shake so that I could hardly hold the opera glass (I was close – but was determined to see – as one should see everything once with attention), the second and third (which shows how dreadfully soon things grow indifferent) I am ashamed to say had no effect on me – as a horror.

Page 26
Why do we punish people?
ACTIVITY You may prefer to use up-to-date examples of real crimes for this Activity. There may well be lots of current examples in the media – today's paper may be teeming with them – that you could use to decide which deserve capital punishment and which do not.

FOCUS TASK A Worksheet 2.14 supports this task, providing a table to complete based on Source B.

Page 27
Christian principles (for punishment)
FOCUS TASK B Worksheet 2.15 supports this with a balancing scales exercise similar to that on Worksheet 2.9.

Pages 28–30
Is life imprisonment a better punishment than hanging?
At the heart of this investigation are the interviews with three women serving life sentences. They were all happy to be interviewed. They laughed a lot and talked about all sorts of issues. Yet at the end the interviewer was free to leave and they were not; it really brought home just what being in prison means, guilty or not.

It may be that the teacher has contact with someone who works in a prison, or someone who is a member of the Board of Visitors or of the Prison Fellowship, or a chaplain. If these people are good at speaking to young people they may be very helpful in exploring this main alternative to capital punishment. Young people tend to assume that life in prison is rosy and an easy alternative. Such speakers might prove the opposite to be true.

Capital punishment review task
Scenario: The British Government is seeking to bring back capital punishment for murderers and terrorists. You are a member of a local Christian ecumenical group which opposes capital punishment.
Your task: To work as a group to research the issue in depth and to produce campaign material that will support your case. You must produce:

- a poster that uses emotive images to get your message across
- a handbill for your churches which encourages members of the congregation to fight against this Bill
- a letter to your MP in which you explain why, as Christians, you cannot support the Bill, and want him to back you.

Here are some Bible passages to consider: Exodus 21.23–25, which makes clear that punishment should not exceed the crime; Matthew 5.38–48, which tells Christians that they should not seek revenge, but even love their enemies; Matthew 26.52, where, at his arrest, Jesus tells those who try to protect him with weapons, that 'those who take the sword will die by the sword'; John 8.1–11, in which Jesus forgives a woman who should have been stoned to death, and tells her to reform her way of life; Romans 12.17–21, where St. Paul teaches about repaying good, not bad, for evil acts.

Page 32
Issues of life and death – review task
Each of Units 2–5 ends with such a review task: a stimulus-based question in examination style.

For these units we have also provided a range of summary worksheets, in a similar style for each unit: **Worksheet 2.16** suggests 'Just a Minute' topics – students have to talk for a minute on a range of life and death issues; **Worksheet 2.17** requires a summary essay which also allows re-evaluation of students' views from the beginning of the unit; **Worksheet 2.18** provides further examination practice using a real past examination question; **Worksheet 2.19** provides Bible 'file cards' for the unit, helping students to learn certain key passages which Christians might apply to issues of life and death; **Worksheet 2.20** is an end of unit test in the form of a quick quiz, for students to test each other or themselves; **Worksheet 2.21** is a word list of key terms used in the unit.

Other review strategies

You might consider:

a) **Creating a comparison chart.** In the first column list issues that you are studying. In the next two or three columns you could summarise contrasting opinions on each issue from different religions that you have studied or from different Christian traditions, and the reasons for the contrasting opinions.

b) **Asking the students to be moral experts.** Introduce to students another contemporary life and death issue which raises similar issues to one that they have come across and ask them, now that they are moral experts, to consider how they could apply Christian teaching to this issue.

For this unit a possible issue for strategy b) would be suicide. Here's a dilemma to consider. A doctor is called to attend someone who has tried to kill himself. The person has left a suicide note. It seems he wanted to die. The doctor arrives before he has died. It is clear to the doctor that the person will die soon if he/she does not take action. What is the doctor's moral responsibility – to let that person die, or to do his/her best to save him?

This was debated recently, following a case when a paramedic had resuscitated a farmer who had tried to kill himself.

Dr Colin Howson suggested that it was not morally permissible to prevent someone from committing suicide.

Here is the reply of Rev. Nick Read, Director of the Rural Stress Network, which specialises in helping people in rural Britain who are feeling suicidal:

'Many people who are suicidal are in an intensely ambivalent state, wanting both to die and to be saved. The statement that "I am going to do it – now" may itself be a desperate plea for help. Provided that the helper has made it clear that they will intervene even against expressed wishes their moral integrity remains intact.'

The Life and Death Machine

1 On your own, add labels to show all the issues that you think this cartoon raises.
2 Many religious people say that some or all of the decisions depicted in the cartoon are not ours to take, and that we should leave these things to God.
  Highlight in one colour all of the issues that you think we should leave to God.
  Highlight in another colour all of the issues that you think we are right to take into our own hands.
3 Add a key to explain your colour coding.
4 Compare and discuss your results with a partner.

Keep this worksheet – you may want to refer to it when you have completed Unit 2.

Christianity in today's world Teacher's Resource Book
© John Murray

Embryology: what the Churches say

Developments in embryology are monitored carefully under very strict regulations by the **Human Fertilisation and Embryology Authority**, which was set up in 1991, following the report of the **Warnock Committee** into this whole issue in 1984.

The Church of England produced a report in 1984 as a response to the Warnock (Human Fertilisation and Embryology) Report. It was published the following year under the title *Personal Origins*. This report was debated by the Synod (the ruling body of the Church of England) and the Synod recommended it, agreeing with much of what the Warnock Report had said.

In 1988 a Private Member's Motion on the issue was debated in the House of Commons and it was agreed as a result that experimentation on 'spare' embryos up until the 14th day after conception was acceptable. The outcome of the debate also emphasised what had been agreed in 1984, that, 'all human life, including life developing in the womb, is created by God in his own image and is therefore to be nurtured, supported and protected'.

The Methodist Church is quite positive about how scientific advances can assist couples in creating babies. Artificial insemination by the husband and IVF are both encouraged as means of helping childless couples, but artificial insemination involving a donor is not seen as acceptable because of problems that it can raise for the child and parents. Research on 'spare' embryos up to 14 days old is seen as permissible since it can be of great help to doctors researching genetic diseases, although the Church teaches that embryos should not be created solely for this purpose.

The Roman Catholic Church takes a rather stricter view on these matters. A document was published in 1987 called *Respect for Human Life in its Origin and the Dignity of Procreation*. This emphasised the principles concerning the sanctity of life laid down much earlier in the *Papal Encyclical, Humanae Vitaea* of 1968. These are, basically, that children are a gift from God, the proper place for whose creation lies in marriage, and whose life begins from the very moment of conception. As a result the Roman Catholic Church will accept artificial insemination and in-vitro fertilisation (IVF) for married couples, provided 'spare' embryos are not created and provided donors are not used to provide sperm or eggs.

The Religious Society of Friends has no authoritative statement about the issue, but seeks always to rejoice in God's creation, and to allow research whilst considering carefully when 'to stop'.

The sanctity of life

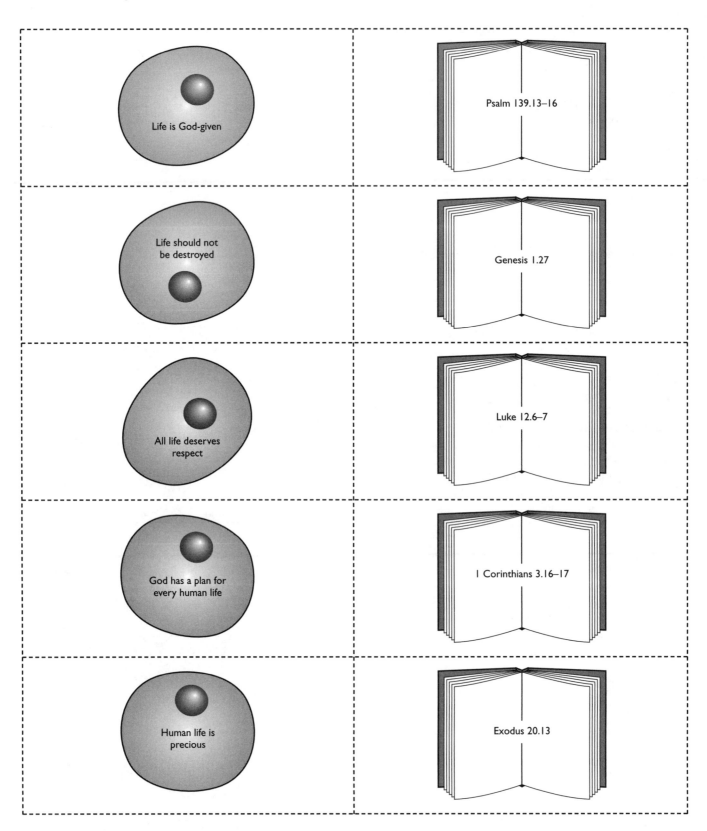

1 Cut out the five 'cells' and the five Bible references.
2 Match up the Bible reference with the idea that it supports.
3 On a large sheet of paper paste down the matched-up pairs.
4 Under each pair write in your own words what that Bible passage says about the idea.
5 Add a large title and some design to complete your poster.

Doctor's Dilemma

You are all young doctors who have just taken your Hippocratic Oath – to do all you can to preserve life. You are looking ahead to your careers. What issues of life and death are you likely to face over the next 40 years? Play this board game to find out. As you progress around the board you will earn or lose points according to how far you have preserved life. Will you retire with a clear conscience?

Rules

Play in a group of four. Throw a dice in turn and move around the board. Each square has plus or minus points. Record your total on the score card below and at the end see which of you has the clearest conscience. Daily Rounds has no score.

Score card

Players' names	Tally plus	Tally minus	Total

Retirement

Scores above 15: You can retire with clear conscience. You have done all that you can to keep the Hippocratic Oath and have made life much pleasanter for many people. Put your feet up with pride.

Scores from 0 to 15: You have worked hard and had the interests of people at heart, although you have faced some tough decisions and not always managed to choose the life-preserving option.

Scores from −15 to −1: You have had a very difficult working life. On many occasions you have been put in a situation where you have had to break the Hippocratic Oath, but you have found this difficult. In the end your concern for people has meant that you have acted out of what you see as compassion.

Scores below −15: You seem to have forgotten what the Hippocratic Oath says. You enjoy 'playing God' and have ignored all ethical codes, seeking only to keep people happy in what they request and using technical advances to create a society of only super-fit and 'wanted' people.

Doctor's Dilemma game board

#	Event	Score
1	Start career.	
2	You save the life of a young boy in a road accident.	+2
3	A teenager wants an abortion. You agree reluctantly.	−2
4	Daily Rounds.	
5	Go on a course to learn about IVF techniques.	+1
6	Cheer up patients by chatting to them.	+1
7	Turn off life-support machine of an overdose victim.	+1
8	Daily Rounds.	
9	You take an extra qualification in gynaecology.	+1
10	Volunteer to join the paramedics in a motorway pile-up.	+3
11	Daily Rounds.	
12	An elderly patient requests euthanasia. You give her husband a strong painkiller and tell him how much to give her.	−2
13	You are asked to witness the execution of a terrorist and to declare death. You cannot do this.	+2
14	You agree to abort a fetus who has Down's Syndrome.	−3
15	Daily Rounds.	
16	A woman with three children asks you to abort one of her unborn, healthy, twins. You refuse.	+3
17	You attend a course about counselling dying patients.	+2
18	A couple are desperate for a child and offer to pay for a surrogate pregnancy. You advise them to try IVF.	+1
19	Daily Rounds.	
20	A routine operation goes wrong and the patient is left in a vegetative state. You tell the family and offer support.	+1
21	The girl who had an abortion as a teenager now finds she is unable to have children naturally. She asks for IVF. You agree.	+2
22	A couple find that their second child is severely handicapped at birth. They ask you not to give it the life-saving operation it needs. You agree.	−4
23	Daily Rounds.	
24	A person with AIDS asks for euthanasia before the disease really gets a hold and it is clear for others to see. You agree.	−3
25	Your hospital is told that it must thaw out frozen unclaimed embryos. You try desperately to contact their 'parents'.	+3
26	An elderly patient with Alzheimer's Disease catches pneumonia. You decide not to administer drugs. She dies.	−2
27	Daily Rounds.	
28	You want to learn more about the hospice movement. Join the support group of your local one.	+3
29	A couple reject their newborn, deformed baby. You advise adoption for it.	+2
30	Retire.	

An abortion survey

Four case studies are described on page 15 of your book.

1 Ask at least 12 people what they think each of the women should do and note their replies on this chart. Use a tick to indicate that the person thinks she should have an abortion and a cross to show that the person thinks she should not. There should be no 'sitting on the fence'.

	Sammi	Mrs O	Mrs P	Ms X	Total ✔	Total ✗
1						
2						
3						
4						
5						
6						
7						
8						
9						
10						
11						
12						

2 Look down the columns. Which case study has the most ticks and which the most crosses?

3 Look across the rows. Are the responses of any of the people you surveyed all ticks or all crosses?

4 What conclusions can you draw from your results about absolute or relative morality? Write your answer here.

_____

_____

_____

_____

5 Explain whether you yourself have relativist or absolutist views on abortion.

_____

_____

_____

_____

When does life begin?

1 Mark in one colour the point on the arrow when you think life begins.
2 Mark in another colour the period when abortion for non-life threatening reasons is legal in Britain.
3 Use a third colour to mark the period when you think abortion should be legal. If you think abortion should never be legal, draw a line at Week 0.
4 Mark with a fourth colour the time at which you think the fetus develops a spirit or a soul. If you do not believe in spirits or souls, do not draw this line.
5 If you have allowed for a spirit or a soul, mark on the diagram of one fetus the place where you think the soul is. Discuss this if you find it difficult.
6 Add a key to explain the significance of all the colours.

Week 0	conception – the sperm and egg join together and grow to form an embryo
Week 4	the heart begins to beat
Week 5	legs and arms begin to form
Week 6	bones begin to form

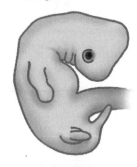

Week 9	the baby begins to look more human and is now called a fetus (or foetus)
Week 12	all organs of the body are formed
Week 14	

Week 20	eyebrows and eyelashes begin to form
Week 23	the fetus can survive outside the mother's body (with medical support)
Week 40	full term – the baby is ready to be born naturally

The development of a baby from conception to birth

Key _____

☐ _____
☐ _____
☐ _____
☐ _____

In this 'think bubble' record your thoughts while you were completing this activity.

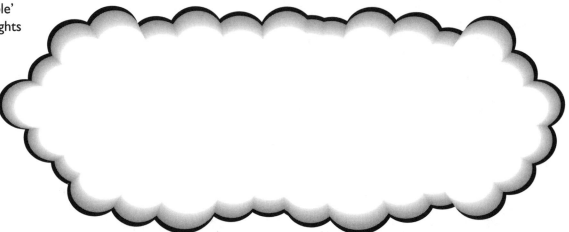

An essay on abortion

The Focus Task on page 19 asks you to write an essay on the topic 'Why do many Christians oppose abortion?' This sheet is to help you gather the information you need, and organise your thoughts.

STAGE 1 Gather your information and evidence

First of all you will need to find the following things from your book or your own notes:

a) What abortion means and when it is legal (see the Checkpoint on page 15).

b) (At least two) arguments used by Christians who would not allow abortion (see page 17, right-hand column, and if you wish Source L on page 18).

c) Two arguments used by Christians who think individuals should decide about abortion (see page 17, left-hand column, and if you wish Sources I or K on page 18).

d) The Bible's principles that form the bases of the views in **b)** and **c)**. For opposing principles see page 14. For a supportive principle see Source F on page 17.

e) Examples of the kinds of authority Christians look to in making these decisions.

STAGE 2 Use your evidence to write draft essay notes

You can use this as an outline for your notes:

Paragraph 1 – Introduction

Abortion is . . .

The Abortion Act says that a woman can have an abortion if . . .

Paragraph 2 – Arguments against abortion

Many Christians oppose abortion. Two reasons which they give for this are . . .

They use the Bible's principle of the sanctity of life to support their views. This means . . .
(Explain this carefully and support it with a Bible reference.)

Paragraph 3 – Arguments for abortion

There are different reasons why some Christians would allow an abortion. Two of these are . . .

They would base their view on the principle in the Bible that . . .

Paragraph 4 – The Bible
(Here you will need to explain, in your own words, that the Bible is not a textbook for Christian living. It does not give specific advice for specific modern situations. Instead it gives principles to guide people. People apply these principles in different ways. Sometimes even the principles themselves seem to conflict with each other.)

Paragraph 5 – Impact on decisions
(Record examples of Christians using different kinds of authority in making their moral decisions.)

Paragraph 6 – My own view

I agree with . . .

because . . .

STAGE 3 Now turn your notes into a full essay

WORKSHEET 2.8

Examination practice: Abortion

Look at Sources J and N on page 18.

a) List and explain three arguments that a supporter of the view shown in photo N might use for abortion. (6)

_____

_____

_____

_____

_____

_____

b) Explain how an opponent, supporting the view shown in picture J, might express her views against abortion. (6)

_____

_____

_____

_____

_____

_____

c) Outline and explain any Bible teaching which you think might help Christians to make a decision on this issue. (6)

_____

_____

_____

_____

_____

_____

d) Do you think that it is possible for Christians to hold an absolutist view against abortion? Show in your answer that you have considered more than one point of view. (6)

_____

_____

_____

_____

_____

_____

_____

The euthanasia balance

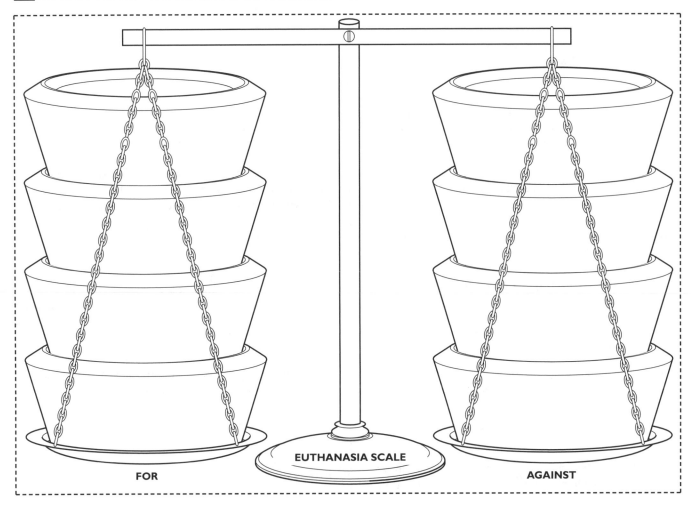

EUTHANASIA SCALE

FOR

AGAINST

1 Cut out the balancing scales and the eight arguments.
2 Paste the balance in the centre of a sheet of paper.
3 Look at each argument. Decide which side of the balance it should go – for or against. Paste them down.
4 Some arguments might seem more important, i.e. weightier, than others. Explain in a sentence which way the balance falls for you.

_____

_____

_____

_____

_____

1 People have been given dominion over other living things by God.	5 Life is sacred. Euthanasia destroys life. So it must be wrong.
2 The Holy Spirit lives in Christians. Euthanasia destroys God's temple. (1 Corinthians 3.16–17)	6 God wants people to have quality of life. If someone has no quality of life euthanasia might be acceptable.
3 There may be a purpose to suffering. People may learn from it.	7 It is more compassionate to care for the dying than to speed up death.
4 People have been given free will by God. They should be able to use this free will to end their own lives.	8 God is love. Stopping suffering is a loving thing to do. So euthanasia could bring more glory to God than keeping a suffering person alive.

WORKSHEET 2.10

A euthanasia debate

1 Killing is always wrong.	**9** God gave doctors the ability to develop the euthanasia drugs. If God had not wanted them to be used then God would not have allowed them to be developed.
2 It happens anyway, so why not legalise it?	**10** We should learn from suffering, not just try to overcome it.
3 We put animals out of their misery, should we not do the same for humans too?	**11** It is impossible to make a euthanasia law that would cover all circumstances.
4 Euthanasia lets the last days of a dying person be planned so he/she can focus on what's important.	**12** People do not make rational decisions under stress.
5 Euthanasia is loving – it puts someone to sleep gently. Love cannot be illegal.	**13** A cure may be found, and then what would we feel about the life we had allowed to end?
6 After what happened in the Holocaust we can never allow euthanasia to become law – we could end up with a second, legal holocaust.	**14** Euthanasia saves money. The money that would be spent on keeping a terminally ill person alive for longer could go on a better cause.
7 All people are of value to God, whatever their ability or disability, so we cannot just end life as if we were throwing away something broken.	**15** Some people have no quality of life.
8 As human beings we have minds which we should use and if that means making the hard decision to end life, we should do it.	**16** We should care better for the dying instead of trying to kill them off.

A day at a hospice

Mary Oates is a Macmillan-trained nurse, who works at a hospice in Essex.

Interviewer (I): How long have you been involved in this kind of work Mary?

Mary Oates (M): I have worked on and off in this area for the last 20 years, although I did stop working full time when my husband and I had our two children.

I: Why do you work at a hospice?

M: For me nursing had always been about improving the quality of people's lives, and working in a hospice is all about that. With my colleagues I try to make people's last few months or weeks as good as they can be. I like working in a separate wing to the hospital wards because here we only have one kind of patient and everyone is in the same boat, so there is opportunity for patients themselves to be supported by other patients.

I: Could you tell us what you do in your job?

M: The team all work different shifts, and the first thing that happens when the team changes over is that we meet together so that we find out about what has happened since we last saw the patients. We can find out medical information through reading the patients' notes, but in a hospice we are dealing with the whole person and so just as important to us is how they and their family are doing mentally. When you are in pain your emotions are really worn down and so for many of our patients their days are full of lows as well as highs. We are there to help them get through their day in whatever way we can. Once we have had our meeting I go and visit the patients I am particularly looking after. There are lots of practical things to deal with so that they do not get bed sores; giving patients their pain killers; taking them to physiotherapy or to one of the activity rooms at the hospice. I use these things as an opportunity to chat to the patients about my day and theirs, and maybe to have a bit of a laugh with them. The image many people have of a hospice is of a quiet place where everyone is quietly dying. Nothing can be further from the truth. I think when you know that you are going to die then you tend to make the most of every opportunity, and if medicine can stop 99% of the pain then death can be faced. We have notes to write up and there isn't a moment of peace in a job like this. Sometimes when a patient is near the end of their life words do not help and sitting holding someone's hand is what I do.

I: What do you like most about your work?

M: Working with people and helping them to die peacefully when the time is right. I like helping the families to get ready for that moment, using past experiences as a way of helping them. I like the fact that my job can make a difference to people's lives. I want them to be spiritually ready for their next life, as well as on good terms with their family.

I: You mention 'spiritually ready', Mary, do you believe in God?

M: Yes I do, and it is that belief that they are going to a better place than this which helps me with my work.

I: What is the worst part of your work?

M: Getting close to patients and really missing them when they do die. It is hard having to be strong when the person has just died and the family is really upset. Sometimes I end up crying with them. I think that tears are good as they show that that person was loved. But it doesn't always help the family to have everyone upset and in a state, so I have to be careful.

I: Why do you think that there are not more hospices?

M: It is strange because in a hospice we can care for patients more cheaply than in a normal hospital ward. Hospices are funded partly by the government, but a lot of money has to be raised by hospices themselves as they are legally charities. This makes it difficult for people to decide to start up a hospice because they have to raise half of the money needed. Local authorities have problems running what they have got without setting up more choices for people. So I think it comes down to money, or a lack of it, in health care.

YOUR TASK

Imagine that you are contributing to a new careers booklet for nurses, covering all aspects of nursing. Use this interview with Mary Oates and the information on page 24 of your book to write a piece under the following headings:

- **What is involved in working in a hospice**
- **The kind of qualities required**

Write no more than 150 words under each heading.

WORKSHEET 2.12

Euthanasia or abortion or both?

In some ways abortion and euthanasia are similar issues; in other ways they are
very different. People sometimes approve of one but not of the other.

For example: Baroness Mary Warnock has chaired a number of committees
which have studied medical ethics. She has a concern for people. She has
spoken openly against abortion. Yet in September 1997 the *Guardian*
newspaper reported that she had admitted to helping her sick husband to die.

Do you think this is inconsistent or do you think it is quite justifiable?

1 Interview (at least) ten people about their views on abortion and euthanasia, and
   see if there is any common pattern.
2 Record their views in this table.
3 Ask people for their reasons and note any relevant comments they make.

	Approves of abortion (Yes/No)	Approves of euthanasia (Yes/No)	Any comments made
1			
2			
3			
4			
5			
6			
7			
8			
9			
10			

4 Write a paragraph explaining your results.

_____

_____

_____

_____

_____

_____

_____

_____

Christianity in today's world Teacher's Resource Book

WORKSHEET 2.13

Examination practice: Euthanasia

Statement A	Statement B
'People have the right to end their own lives when they wish.' (from a Humanist statement on euthanasia)	'If better methods were developed to care for the dying, euthanasia would not be needed.' (from a Methodist statement on euthanasia)

a) State and explain **two** religious reasons why some Christians disagree with Statement A. (4)

i) _____

_____

_____

ii) _____

_____

_____

b) State and explain **three** circumstances in which euthanasia is regarded by some people as acceptable. (6)

i) _____

_____

_____

ii) _____

_____

_____

iii) _____

_____

_____

c) Do you agree or disagree with Statement B? Give reasons for your answer. (3)

_____

_____

_____

_____

NEAB (GCSE short course) RE Syllabus D, Paper 2, 1997

WORKSHEET **2.13** (continued)

Model answer: Euthanasia

a) Two religious reasons why Christians might disagree with Statement A:

i) It is not up to individuals to end their lives when they wish, as their lives are not their own. The Bible makes it clear that all life was given by God, only God should have the right to take it away.

ii) It is being very selfish to want to end your own life in your own time. People are not islands, we live in families and to simply decide to end your life would cause immense distress for your family.

b) Three circumstances in which euthanasia is regarded by some people as acceptable:

i) If an elderly person who is senile and a burden on her family gets a disease it may be fairer on all concerned to let her die peacefully rather than treat the disease.

ii) If a badly handicapped baby is born it is kinder to the baby to let it die rather than live a short and painful life, and more compassionate to the parents who would grow to love it before it died, and may have to give up their whole life to care for it.

iii) If a young person is severely injured by a road accident and will spend the rest of his life in great pain, unable to communicate with friends and family, it seems more compassionate to let him die rather than lose all that he once had.

c) Do you agree or disagree with Statement B? Give reasons for your answer.

I agree with Statement B. It is possible today to care for the dying in hospices. Special drugs can control their pain. In a hospice people and their families come to terms with dying so they can die happy and still feel in control of their own lives. These hospices can do away with the need for euthanasia. In the Bible Jesus said, 'I have come that you may have life, life in all its fullness.' I think that by this he meant that we should live life to the very end, and hospices can help us to do just that.

or

I disagree with Statement B. However good the care of the dying is, there would still be a need for euthanasia. Some people will still ask to die. It may be that they are thinking not just of themselves, but also of their families. They do not like to see their family suffer. Also, care of the dying will always be expensive. We should not be wasting money on people who want to die, but we should spend it on caring for those who will live.

Christianity in today's world Teacher's Resource Book © John Murray

Does capital punishment help?

This table lists the reasons for punishment from Source B on page 26.

1 In the second column, for each reason explain whether capital punishment can achieve that purpose, and why/why not.
2 In the third column, explain whether life imprisonment can achieve that purpose, and why/why not.

Keep this table – you will need it later.

Reason to punish	Can capital punishment achieve that purpose? (Explain why/why not)	Can life imprisonment achieve that purpose? (Explain why/why not)
deterrence – to discourage the offender (and other potential offenders) from committing similar crimes		
protection – for the safety of society, individuals in it, and sometimes the offender themselves		
reform – to help the offender to become a 'better' person		
retribution – revenge for those who have been wronged		
reparation – to allow the criminal to 'pay' for what they have done and have their guilt wiped out so they can make a fresh start		
vindication – to show that the authority of the law is being upheld – to ensure that people respect the law		

The capital punishment balance

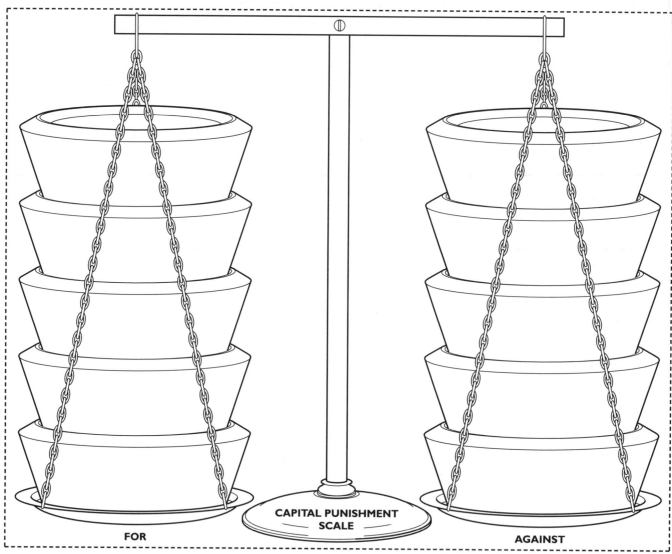

CAPITAL PUNISHMENT SCALE

FOR   AGAINST

1 It is cheaper than life imprisonment.	**2** Mistakes can be made. The innocent could be executed.
3 It makes the murderer a martyr.	**4** It does not allow for forgiveness or reform.
5 The Old Testament taught 'an eye for an eye'. This means a death for a death.	**6** It shows society's condemnation of the crime.
7 Jesus forgave someone who should have been stoned to death.	**8** It does not work. Capital punishment does not bring down murder rates.
9 It deters potential murderers.	**10** An executed murderer cannot kill again.

1 Cut out the balancing scales and the ten arguments.
2 Paste the balance in the centre of a sheet of paper.
3 Look at each argument. Decide which side of the balance it should go – for or against. Paste them down.
4 Decide which arguments you consider weightier, then explain in a sentence which way the balance falls for you.

WORKSHEET 2.16

Just a Minute: Life issues

Note to teachers:

1 Copy and cut out the statements on this sheet.
2 Give each student one of the statements.
3 Ask the students to prepare notes which will enable them to speak in support of their statement for at least one minute, with no pauses! They should try to include relevant Christian teachings or ideas too. If they disagree with the statement it should not matter – they can put their own views afterwards.

1 A childless couple should simply accept their situation – there must be a reason for it.	**8** No woman has an excuse for getting pregnant by accident.
2 Doctors may be well trained, but they should not have the right to play God.	**9** Handicapped children can be very loving and give great joy. They should not be deprived of the right to life.
3 God gave doctors the skill to develop modern life-saving and destroying techniques, so they should continue to develop such practices.	**10** A person who is making no contribution to society, just lying in a hospital bed, should be allowed to die.
4 It is good to research on 'spare' embryos as it might lead to a cure for some diseases.	**11** A cure might be found for cancer, or AIDS, then can you bring back those who have been made to die early through euthanasia?
5 Every embryo and fetus is a miniature human being.	**12** Murderers, who have shown no respect for the life of others, do not deserve to live themselves.
6 The Christian marriage service should not include prayers for children to be born into the marriage, as it places unfair expectations on a couple.	**13** Killing another in the name of the law can never be justified – we stoop to the depth of the murderer.
7 Abortion is the only compassionate response to an unwanted pregnancy.	**14** All life is God-given and sacred.

WORKSHEET **2.17**

Issues of life and death: Re-evaluation

This sheet is to review your work on Unit 2.

Look back to your answers to Worksheet 2.1. Have your views changed at all in the light of what you have studied? Reflect on your views and complete the following 'think bubbles'.

I think sanctity of life means

To me quality of life is

The decisions on life that I think should be left to God are

The decisions about life and death that I think people should take are

For me, the most difficult life decision is

Now use your thoughts, and all that you have learned in Unit 2, to write an essay:

> **Jesus said, 'I have come that you may have life, life in all its fullness' (John 10.10). How does this saying of Jesus apply to issues of life and death in the world today?**

Use the following headings to structure your essay:

Introduction (which issues of life and death are you going to consider?)
Fullness of life (is this a measure of quantity or quality?)
One Christian application of this principle
A different Christian application
My own views (with reasons)
Conclusion (how far this is a useful principle to apply to modern issues)

Christianity in today's world Teacher's Resource Book © John Murray

WORKSHEET 2.18

Examination practice: Issues of life and death

Abortion
Capital Punishment
Euthanasia

a) Choose **one** of the topics listed above. For the topic you have chosen describe **one** situation in which Christians might **oppose** the taking of a human life. Give reasons for their opposition including at least **one** biblical passage which you have studied. (6)

_____

_____

_____

_____

_____

_____

b) Using any **two** of the topics listed above, describe **two** different situations when Christians might **accept** the taking of a human life. For **each** situation explain why a Christian might accept it. (8)

_____

_____

_____

_____

_____

_____

_____

_____

_____

c) Do you think that Christians treat human life with more respect than non-Christians? Give reasons for your answer, showing that you have considered more than one point of view. (6)

_____

_____

_____

_____

_____

_____

_____

NEAB (GSCE full course) RE Syllabus B, Paper 2A, 1996

Bible file cards: Issues of life and death

In your exam you will improve your grade if you can use Bible references to support your explanation of important Christian principles.

Cut out and keep these file cards. They should help you remember some useful and important passages. Use the blanks to record other passages, e.g. Matthew 5.38–42.

Remember, however, that Christians don't believe something because there is one text in the Bible that says it. They look for Bible *principles*. The text is only important as an example of a Bible principle.

> **Note to teachers:**
>
> You may wish to enlarge this sheet to A3 when photocopying, to make the file cards a more manageable size.

LIFE AND DEATH

Reference: Genesis 1.27

Context: OT – Creation story

Summary: God makes humans 'in His own image'

Application: Humans made by God so God's property; killing human means killing part of God

---

LIFE AND DEATH

Reference: Psalm 139.13–16

Context: OT – Psalmist speaking to God

Summary: God knows all about us even before we are born; God created each person

Application: All are unique, gifts of God; killing a person is killing something God has deliberately called into being

---

LIFE AND DEATH

Reference: Exodus 20.13

Context: OT – one of Ten Commandments

Summary: Do not kill

Application: When given it meant pre-meditated killing, not war; clear respect for life from God

---

LIFE AND DEATH

Reference: John 10.10b

Context: NT – Jesus speaking

Summary: I have come that you may have life, life in all its fullness

Application: Quality v. quantity of life; value of all; getting the most out of life; life is a gift from God

---

LIFE AND DEATH

Reference: Luke 12.6–7

Context: NT – Jesus to disciples

Summary: God values sparrows; you are worth more than many sparrows

Application: Humans are special to God, none should be injured in any way

---

LIFE AND DEATH

Reference: Romans 12.14–21

Context: NT – Paul in letter

Summary: Do not repay evil with evil

Application: Value of all life; no one has right to play God; capital punishment is wrong

---

LIFE AND DEATH

Reference:

Context:

Summary:

Application:

LIFE AND DEATH

Reference:

Context:

Summary:

Application:

End of Unit Quiz: Issues of life and death

Test yourself or your neighbour with this quick quiz.

1 What is IVF?

2 What does the word *sacred* mean?

3 Write out one Bible passage that might be used by Christians to show that all life is sacred.

4 What does the abortion law say about the abortion of handicapped fetuses?

5 What does it say about 'social' abortions?

6 State two arguments that Christians might use *for* abortion.

7 State two arguments that they might use *against* it.

8 At what date after conception does the human heart start beating?

9 Name the 1968 Roman Catholic document which opposes abortion.

10 What is the sixth of the Ten Commandments?

11 Which Christian MP introduced the Abortion Bill in 1967?

12 What does the word *euthanasia* mean?

13 Name a pro-euthanasia group.

14 What does the Hippocratic Oath, taken by all doctors, state?

15 State two arguments used by Christians to support euthanasia.

16 State two arguments against it.

17 What is the hospice movement?

18 What did Jesus teach about life in John 10.10b?

19 Is capital punishment still legal in the UK?

20 List four purposes of punishment.

21 On what Old Testament passage do many people base their belief in capital punishment as revenge?

22 State two arguments used in favour of capital punishment.

23 List two arguments used specifically by Christians against it.

24 Suggest one Bible passage which is opposed to capital punishment.

25 What attitude do many Christians advocate towards offenders?

Word list: Issues of life and death

You need to know all of these words and their meanings.

Abortion   The unnatural termination of a fetus before it has reached full term in the womb

Birth control   Control of conception, and therefore of births

Capital punishment   The death penalty

Conception   The moment when a woman's egg is fertilised

Contraceptive   Device 'against conception'

Deter   To prevent someone from doing something by punishing other wrong-doers as an example

Embryo   The name for a developing baby (fetus) during the first 9 weeks after conception

Euphemism   A nice way of phrasing something unpleasant

Euthanasia   To allow someone to die when they are suffering and will die soon anyway

Family planning   Natural and artificial methods that allow couples to plan when to have children

Fatal   Leads to death

Fetus   'Baby' developing in the womb

Illegitimacy   Being born without father and mother being married to each other

Justice   Seeing that right is done by someone

Legalisation   Making something legal/allowed by law

Mandatory   Something you must do by law

Murder   An act in which a sane person kills another person, provided they die within a year and a day

Permissive   Allowing an immoral lifestyle

Quality   Value, goodness of something

Quantity   Length, amount of time

Reform   To change a person for the better

Reparation   Making amends/paying for wrong-doing

Repentance   Realising you have done wrong, apologising and being determined not to do it again

Retribution   Paying back for something done to you

Revenge   Getting your own back

Sanctity   Specialness, holiness

Termination   Ending

Viability   The likelihood that a fetus could survive apart from its mother if born early

Vindication   Seeing that the law is upheld

Voluntary   When an individual decides to do something

UNIT 3
Relationships

Overview

This unit focuses on human relationships: marriage, sex, divorce, discrimination, racism, sexism, service to and respect for others. These are wide-ranging issues. In the NEAB Syllabus D the compulsory area is 'Sex, marriage and divorce', although this may change with time.

Starting strategies

Page 33

The cartoon is to encourage students to think about relationships in the broadest sense – to look beyond friends to a much wider group with whom they have a relationship: teachers, local shopkeepers, MP, and so on. It might be useful to discuss how these more distant relationships differ from the friendship models.

3.1 The perfect relationship?

Page 34

ACTIVITY The Either/Or task is to allow for students to opt for a safer alternative which does not expose their own relationships to close scrutiny. In task 1 you could substitute other pictures of your own that show a moment of tension in a relationship.

If students opt for task 2 they should be accorded space and privacy. Some may not wish to share their responses with a partner.

An additional line of questioning for part a) would be which of the relationships their parents (or others) might regard as good or bad. How do they handle these opinions?

A lot of discussion can arise from either of these tasks but, for the purposes of the unit, task 3 is the most important element. The list of qualities that arises could be kept and referred back to as other aspects of relationships are considered through the rest of the unit.

Worksheet 3.1 supports students in this task by suggesting certain qualities for them to prioritise. It also adds rogue characteristics for them to reject. You could narrow the focus: for example, which qualities are needed for a marriage; for a boyfriend/girlfriend relationship; for family relationships, etc.

3.2 Are Christian ideas about marriage out of date?

After a starter quiz the unit then deals with the topic in the broad categories of sex (pages 36–7), marriage (pages 38–9), family life (pages 40–42) and divorce (pages 43–4).

There are a number of useful videos which are good as starters or to mix in with material from the book. CARE produce a pack called *Make Love Last*, which is about abstinence education and is well produced. The BBC *Words into Action* series has *Love*, and the *RE Collection* has *In Sickness and in Health*. The teacher needs to remember that the aim here is to look at what different Christians believe; it is not to provide sex education.

Page 35

ACTIVITY This quiz is designed to be fun, but also to make a serious point. An attitude scale is provided on **Worksheet 3.2**, but it would be worthwhile for the students to devise their own scoring scheme in order to encourage deeper consideration of the answers.

Page 36

What is sex for?

SOURCE A We have deliberately chosen a free paraphrase of The Song of Songs which could be compared with a more literal Bible translation (Song of Songs 5.10–16).

Worksheet 3.3 provides an additional discussion-based activity: What is sex? adapted from the pack mentioned above, *Make Love Last*.

Page 37

Why do many Christians keep sex for marriage?

SAVE AS ... **Worksheet 3.4** provides a large copy of Source D which could be copied onto OHT and used for class discussion or for students to annotate. It can be re-used later for the major task on Worksheet 3.7.

Pages 38–9

What is a Christian marriage?

In this course the wedding service is only worth a focus for what it tells us about Christian ideas about marriage. Students will not get GCSE marks for simply knowing what happens at a Christian wedding! They will get marks for knowing *why* these things happen.

SAVE AS ... As a follow-up to task 1, students could write their own ideal marriage service – what would they keep, delete or adapt from the outline in Source F?

A powerful song celebrating an alternative to a church wedding is Sting's *Secret Marriage* on *Nothing like the Sun*, 1987, from A and M Records.

Pages 40–41

Family values

The focus of the investigation is values but there are many other issues that are raised by the spread: the use of Sunday; spending time together; the use of the Bible; baptism; spending money.

Page 41
FOCUS TASK For task 2, stress that a written description of their cartoons is adequate.

Page 42
Pressures on family life

CHECKPOINT Don't miss the details about contraception here, as they are quite central for some syllabuses.

ACTIVITY **Worksheet 3.5** supports this television survey.

Pages 43–4
When marriages fail

This explores Christian options when marriage breaks down and the diversity of opinions about divorce. Obviously this is a topic that requires tact in the classroom. Many of the students may have first-hand experience of the breakdown of their own parents' marriages.

Marriage to one person for life is the Christian ideal. However, many denominations recognise that in the modern world this has just not been possible for many couples, even those who profess to be Christians. We need to remember that historically marriage 'for life' was a relatively short time. With the development of modern medical care and better standards of living people are living longer and marriage for life may now be for a very long time! Students could discuss this issue and consider whether the Churches need to change their thinking about marriage in the light of the contemporary situation – a discussion point raised by question 5 on page 44.

It is interesting that the Government, in its recently published document on *Values in the Curriculum*, missed out marriage from the first draft but was persuaded to add the concept of marriage following pressure from religious groups in the original discussion forum.

Page 43
FOCUS TASK The subject of task 5 is a required topic in some syllabuses, so once again don't miss it.

Worksheet 3.6 summarises the different views of the different Churches on divorce and remarriage, and provides a cloze letter-writing exercise to reinforce those different views.

Page 44
ACTIVITY You could also suggest that they consider what to do with the wedding ring(s).

FOCUS TASK **Worksheet 3.7** suggests an alternative major task which can bring together all the students' work on sex, marriage and divorce. This will be good for revision purposes.

Worksheet 3.8 provides examination practice on marriage and divorce. The continuation sheet gives suggested answer guidelines.

3.3 Why do Christians disagree about homosexuality?

Sexuality is a sensitive subject in the classroom, and homosexuality particularly so. There are also legal issues to bear in mind when dealing with this investigation in the classroom – teachers should be aware that it is illegal to be found to be promoting homosexual practice.

As the investigation makes clear, Christians can have strongly opposing views on this matter. Teachers and students do too. When a range of teachers were asked to comment on this material, some regarded it as far too pro-gay for them to use; others regarded it as far too anti-gay for them to use!

Since this is not a prescribed topic in NEAB Syllabus D it can be freely skipped over. However, before you take that easy option let us explain what we have tried to achieve in the investigation. We have tried to combine a study of contemporary Christian views (pages 45–7) with a detailed look at a biblical text at the heart of the issue (page 48). As well as reflecting on the nature of relationships from a different perspective, this investigation should also raise all sorts of questions about the nature of biblical authority, a very important point which might be particularly stimulating for more able students.

Worksheet 3.9 develops further this idea of the contrasting interpretations of the Bible; **Worksheet 3.10** encourages balanced note-taking about this issue.

Another useful resource to use for this topic might be a BBC *Everyman* documentary *Simon's Cross*, shown a few years ago, about a gay Anglican priest (Simon Bailey) with AIDS working in a pit village in South Yorkshire. It highlights the different views that people had about him in the parish. It needs to be viewed by the teacher first and used selectively so as not to give the impression that all gay men have AIDS, but it is very powerful. Simon also wrote a book of prayers for Church House Publishing, *Still with God*, which some groups might like to read. Simon died in 1996.

3.4 How do Christians respond to racism?

Churches in Britain have been concerned about the problems of racism for many years. This unit begins with an example of how the Church has responded to these problems. As the unit develops it argues that Christians have not been blameless when it comes to racism (pages 50–51). Pages 52–3 look at how British churches are dealing with the problems of racism today.

Page 49
CHECKPOINT The distinction between prejudice and discrimination is a favourite examination question.

Worksheet 3.12 helps firm up the distinction through some more examples; it is intended for use with question 6 on page 52.

Page 50

What do Christians believe about racism?

ACTIVITY A **Worksheet 3.11** is a writing frame for the letter to the DRC.

Page 51

Images of Jesus

There are plenty of other images which could be used, including a number elsewhere in the Student's Book – see, for example, page 87. You might want to tease out question 1 into more detailed image analysis. You could give students a large image in the centre of a page and ask them to annotate it to show what it says about Jesus. A series of questions around the picture could help their thinking, e.g.

- Think of a caption for this picture.
- What is Jesus doing?
- Look at Jesus' face and try, if possible, to describe his feelings.
- How are colours used in the picture?
- Are there any significant shapes or features in the background you can comment on?
- Where is the scene taking place?
- Do you think the setting is important?
- How do other people in the picture react to Jesus?

Then the students could summarise underneath: 'The impression I get of Jesus from this picture is .... I think this is because ....'

Pages 52–3

Challenging racism in British Churches

The reports of Churches Minorities Ethnic Anglican Concerns: *Seeds of Hope and the Passing Winter* make interesting reading and are available from Church House Bookshop (31 Great Smith Street, London SW1P 3BN, 0171 340 0276).

If it is possible students might benefit from discussions with Christians from other minority ethnic groups to broaden the case studies.

Page 53

FOCUS TASK **Worksheet 3.13** supports the writing of this policy.

3.5 Are women treated as equals in Christianity?

The first three pages (54–6) use women's ordination as priests as an extended case study. The investigation then broadens into a more general survey of attitudes towards women in the Church (pages 57–9).

Teachers interested in taking these issues further may find two books useful: *Sexism and God Talk* by Rosemary Radford Ruether (SCM 1983) and *What will happen to God?* by William Oddie (SPCK 1984). The book mentioned on page 59, *Women at the Well*, is edited by Kathleen Fischer (SPCK 1989).

It might be interesting to invite in local women priests or men who oppose them, but the lessons would need to be set up very carefully to avoid stereotyping or unpleasant experiences for either side. Perhaps a way of using visitors in this investigation might be to ask students to prepare questions for speakers in advance, which are then vetted by staff and passed to the visitors prior to the visit.

Note that the issue of gender-biased language is raised on page 57. You may notice that throughout the book we have studiously avoided using gender pronouns for God. It might produce some grammatical oddities but we think it is worth the effort. See if your students notice.

Pages 54–6

Women and the priesthood

The debate suggested on page 56 is the focus of this material. The 'Save As' task on page 54, the questions on page 55 and Sources A–F will yield a wide range of evidence and attitudes for the students to use in their debate. They should also feel free to raid the second half of the investigation (pages 57–9) for ideas on either side of the debate.

One mechanism for getting the debate going would be to gather as many statements as possible from the book and arrange them around the room; then ask students to look at them all and to note down the ones with which they most agree, or to stand near them.

Page 56

DISCUSS Another scruples-type scenario might also help here: Jane has recently been appointed as the vicar of a small town church. At the end of the service a young couple come up to her and explain that they will not be coming to this church any more because the Bible says that women should not be priests. If you were Jane, what would you do? What would you say to the couple?

Pages 57–9

Are women and men equal in the sight of God?

The many Sources on page 57, and possibly others from elsewhere in this investigation, could be copied and arranged by students in a diamond shape, the most sexist at the top and the least sexist at the bottom, with the others as appropriate in between. This task stimulates interesting debate as well as drawing out how students understand the term 'sexism'. It is, of course, a rather subjective exercise and comparison with others would be needed.

Page 59

FOCUS TASK Task 3 is a demanding essay-writing task. **Worksheet 3.14** provides a writing frame and guidance on preparing for the essay for less able students.

Worksheet 3.15 provides examination practice on prejudice and discrimination.

<u>3.6</u> How can Christians serve others?

This final investigation in the unit covers what NEAB Syllabus D calls 'The individual in society', which embraces service to fellow human beings, respect for authority and work towards justice and peace. These are fundamental themes which necessarily overlap with many others through the book.

Page 60

Serve those in need . . .

ACTIVITY Worksheet 3.16 supports this Activity.

Page 61

And respect authority . . .

Whom do Christians obey, and whom should they respect? These are and have been very real problems for all Christians throughout the centuries. For the first Christians, whom they served – God or man – was a life-threatening decision. Most students, if they have lived in modern Britain all their lives, might need help in understanding how decisions could cost such a lot.

Question 1 This asks students to think about whom they obey or respect in their lives and why. Be prepared for students who say 'no-one' – this is not a truthful response as they will respect certain media/music/sports people if no-one else! **Worksheet 3.17** supports this task.

FOCUS TASK Examples given earlier in the book that you could consider include Christians supporting the Ogunwobi family and Christians opposing the apartheid regime in South Africa. Other possible stories which could help students in this task are:

a) **Corrie Ten Boom** and her family, who hid Jews in their house in Holland and helped them to escape to freedom, disobeying the Nazi government by doing this.
b) **Brother Andrew** who used to smuggle Bibles into communist countries although they were declared illegal by the government.
c) **Christians in Russia** before the fall of communism, who used to meet illegally to study the Bible and to pray together.

If these stories are unfamiliar then teachers might use their own knowledge, or ask a local Christian leader to provide some.

The story of the Orthodox Church in Russia and Eastern Europe provides a useful example. Almost all the countries where the Orthodox Church is strongest were for much of the 20th century ruled by communist governments, strongly opposed to Christianity.

Communists see religion as an illusion. In revolutionary Russia they also saw it as the way the state had in the past controlled ordinary people and made them accept awful conditions. The new communist governments in Russia and Eastern Europe were therefore very eager to stamp out religion. Many churches were closed, priests were murdered, religious literature was banned, training colleges for priests were closed, etc. At the religious level, the communist ideology that focused so much on the material (money, things) was far divorced from the Orthodox mentality which was much more concerned with transcendence and symbolism.

Orthodox historians describe the life of the Church under communism as being a 'shaking out'. Being a Christian in a communist state involved a real sacrifice. Most notably it prevented you getting a good job – practising Christians were regarded with suspicion – and it prejudiced the progress of your children in education or at work. Despite this, or even because of this, the Orthodox Church remained strong. They say it shook out the half-hearted, tore out the dead wood. Only the really committed stayed within the Church. Some Orthodox Christians 'went underground'. They continued to worship, but on their own or in one another's homes if their churches had been closed. The communists allowed 55 churches to be maintained in Moscow, where there were more than seven million people. These churches were always full.

The Orthodox Church in Russia did not see it as their role to criticise the state. Instead they saw their role as living a life of Christian self-sacrifice and self-denial – showing the silent power of love – within a state that otherwise was brutal and materialistic. However, many Russian émigrés who fled communist rule were bitterly critical of the Russian Orthodox Church for not resisting the state. They accused it of 'selling out' to communism.

Pages 62–3

Liberation Theology

There is a useful section on Liberation Theology in Brazil on the BBC video *Christianity in Today's World: Christianity in a Material World*, which would be good to show at this point.

There is an issue of violence related to Liberation Theology, which we have covered separately on page 87 of the Student's Book. However, Liberation Theology is not primarily about violence but about politics and the struggle for justice. Christians who believe in a God of love and justice find they have to get involved in politics to achieve change. The poor and down-trodden find that according to the Bible God is on the side of the oppressed and powerless, not on the side of the powerful or the oppressors. They gain support and comfort from that. It offers them a biblical basis for their political struggle.

Page 62

Question 3 Romero meant that probably no-one would care about the thousands of peasants who were killed for disagreeing with the government, but people outside of El Salvador would notice and be shocked by priests being murdered by the government because they sided with the peasants. Their deaths would also show that the

Church was standing up for righteousness and showing up how evil the government was in El Salvador.

Page 63

Source K tells a highly abbreviated story of Oscar Romero's life. A full-length video feature is available from video stores and is also on TV from time to time if you prefer to show this to students.

FOCUS TASK This applies the issue to the UK. The two quotes are necessarily quite bald in order to help students reach their own view on how Christians work out their spiritual and political roles. There is much more discussion material available. One example is the book *Talking Heads* by J. John and Sue Cavill which includes an interview with Simon Hughes, Christian MP:

'I believe we live in an unfair world and I want to make it fairer. I get angry and impatient at its unfairness, and that's what brought me to politics.

'The Christian gospel does not prescribe specific political remedies; it prescribes principles of justice and ordering the world, and I clearly believe that some political views and activities and positions are less compatible with those than others. But it is clear that there are Christians in all parties, and that will always be so.

'It's not Christian to have as a specific consequence of policy that the gap between the rich and the poor widens. It's not Christian to encourage the creation of personal wealth to the detriment of other people's survival. It's not Christian to spend little on our duties to the much poorer people of the world, when we are so rich.

'I don't think Jesus would have belonged to a political party. You can't appeal to everybody if you start off from being in a select organisation. Christ clearly came to give a message which was above politics. My security isn't in my politics: being a Christian gives me principles which my politics by definition can't give. Political parties change positions. My Christian faith is fundamentally unchanging.'

Worksheet 3.18 provides examination practice on 'The individual in society'.

Page 64

This is an end of unit review task.
Worksheet 3.19 provides Bible file cards for the unit; **Worksheet 3.20** is an end of unit test; **Worksheet 3.21** is the word list for the unit.

Another review strategy

You could again ask the students to be 'moral experts' (see page 29 of this Resource Book for a general note about this). A worthwhile topic would be a story of bullying. How can Christian principles about relationships be applied to bullying?

WORKSHEET 3.1

A good relationship

1 Cut out these cards.
2 Check that you know what each word means. If you don't, look it up in a dictionary.
3 Discard those that you do not think are characteristics of a good relationship. Keep those that you think are.
4 Prioritise those that you have kept – put the most important qualities at the top.
5 Explain your order to a partner.

Love	Anger	Shared beliefs about God
Commitment	Guilt	Responsibility
Honesty	Bitterness	Faithfulness
Trust	Revenge	Selflessness
Acceptance	Forgiveness	Loyalty
Time together	Shared interests	Stewardship
Listening	Compatibility	Respect

Christianity in today's world Teacher's Resource Book © John Murray

<u>**A**re you the marrying kind? Attitude scale</u>

How did you get on in the Quick Quiz on page 35? Work out your score using the table below, then add up your total and see where you are on the marriage scale below.

Score table

	a)	b)	c)	d)
1.	a) 3	b) 1	c) 2	d) 0
2.	a) 1	b) 2	c) 0	d) 3
3.	a) 1	b) 3	c) 0	d) 2
4.	a) 0	b) 1	c) 3	d) 2
5.	a) 3	b) 1	c) 2	d) 0
6.	a) 3	b) 2	c) 1	d) 0
7.	a) 1	b) 2	c) 3	d) 0
8.	a) 3	b) 1	c) 2	d) 0
9.	a) 1	b) 3	c) 2	d) 0

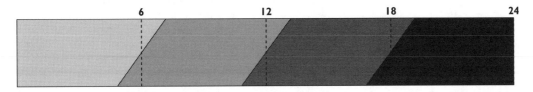

I can't cope with commitment
You are definitely not the marrying kind! In fact, you are not very interested in relationships at all.

Relationships – yes! Marriage – no!
Relationships are important to you but, for whatever reason, you don't like the idea of marrying. You may even think that marriage gets in the way of a good relationship. You show your commitment to people in other ways.

I'm the marrying kind!
You believe in marriage – but you like to keep a level head. You know marriages can go wrong, but you still feel that marriage is a good way of expressing love and commitment.

Get me to the altar quick!
You'd feel at home in *Brides* magazine. Love and marriage are the focus of your life. You won't rest until you've found 'the right one'.

Do you think this score is an accurate assessment of your own attitude to marriage? Explain your answer.

_____

_____

_____

_____

_____

_____

WORKSHEET **3.3**

What is sex?

1 Look at the list of remarks about sex below. Circle your 'top ten'.
2 Work out the overall top five and bottom five for the whole class.
3 Discuss what these choices say about your own class's view of sex.

the ultimate expression of love	the most intimate relationship
for making babies	a force so powerful it is amazing
an exciting tease	painful
temptation	complete surrender to someone else
exciting, but over quickly	all-consuming fire
just a relief of a biological urge	a lifelong commitment
a delicious game	part of a whole relationship
romantic attraction	the start of a new life
the best thing since sliced bread	hidden but always there
the fullest expression of friendship	dirty
nice when it's naughty	becoming an adult
orgasm	a basic necessity
fun	four minutes
a way to get real satisfaction	better each time
full and deep trust	not as good as it's made out to be
complete letting go	for marriage

Christianity in today's world Teacher's Resource Book   © John Murray

Why do many Christians keep sex for marriage?

The diagram shows some positive reasons why many Christians keep sex for marriage.
Write on it an explanation of each reason in your own words.

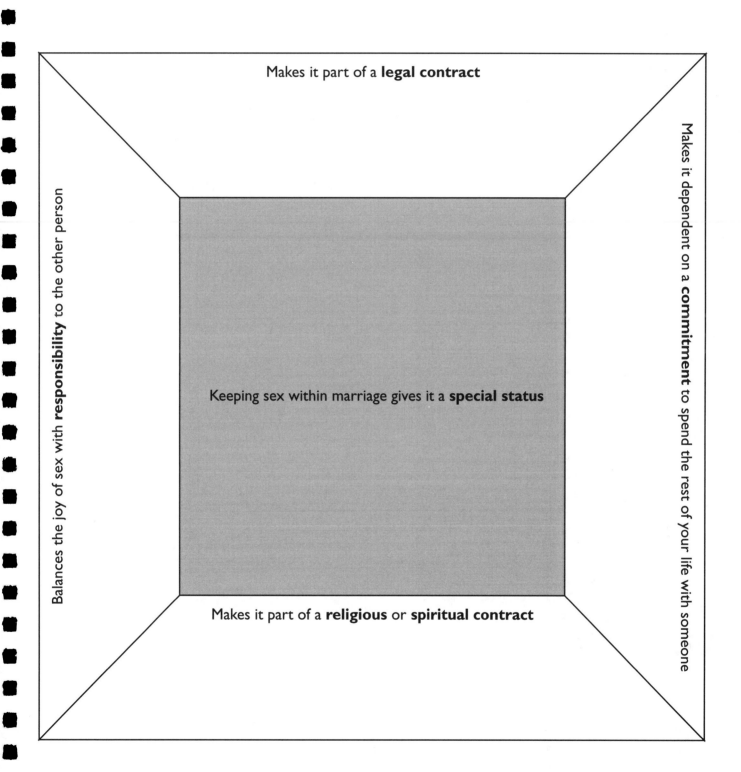

Makes it part of a **legal contract**

Makes it dependent on a **commitment** to spend the rest of your life with someone

Balances the joy of sex with **responsibility** to the other person

Keeping sex within marriage gives it a **special status**

Makes it part of a **religious** or **spiritual contract**

Television survey

1 Watch an evening's soap operas and advertisements on television. As you do so, complete the chart below. For each programme, put a tick in the second column if the Christian values in the first column are shown, and a cross if they are not. Use the third column to jot down examples.

2 Compare your chart with those of others in your class and discuss how the media today presents family life. Do you agree with the values that are being presented?

Values	Present ✔ or absent ✗	Comment or examples
forgiveness		
acceptance of people as they are		
thinking of others before self		
honesty		
sharing God together		
trust		
spending time together		
sharing material and emotional things		

Christianity in today's world Teacher's Resource Book   © John Murray

Remarriage in church?

Different traditions see remarriage of divorced people in church differently.

The Roman Catholic Church will not allow remarriage because it does not accept divorce. The marriage vows are made for life and therefore even a civil, legal divorce is not recognised. Marriage is a sacrament and cannot be broken, so obviously there cannot be any remarriage. A marriage may be annulled (a bishop agrees that the marriage never really took place in the start), but that is difficult and rare.

Other Protestant Churches will sometimes remarry people, although usually only those who regularly attend their church. Some ministers believe that it is more compassionate to give people a second chance and so they will remarry anyone.

The Church of England rarely allows remarriage, although it does see civil divorces as valid and will bless a couple after a service in a Register Office. After a long debate by the General Synod, remarriage is now occasionally allowed, at the discretion of the minister, but permission from a bishop cannot be given.

The Orthodox Church believes the Church has the authority to grant divorces, as it is the Church which marries the couple. Sometimes there is a special service. Remarriage is allowed in church, but it is not as lively a service as a first marriage ceremony.

You are a Christian couple who want to marry in church. One of you has been divorced from a previous marriage partner. You have written to each of your local churches asking them to marry you in church. On the second sheet, complete each of their different responses, paying careful attention to their reasons.

Remarriage in church? Response letters

Read the information on the first sheet. Then complete these letters from the different ministers.

Dear

Thank you for your letter asking that I marry you in the Catholic Church. I am afraid that I _____ marry you. This is because _____ _____ _____.

In the Catholic Church marriage is seen as a _____ and as such it cannot be broken. Technically one of you is still _____.

Yours

Dear

Thank you for your letter asking that I marry you in the Church of England. I am afraid that I _____ marry you.
If I were to ask my _____ for permission he would refuse it because _____ _____.

I am sorry, but I am very happy to give you a _____ following a register office ceremony.

Yours

Dear

Thank you for your letter asking that I marry you in the Methodist Church. I am pleased to say that I _____ marry you. My church would love to welcome you because _____ _____.

Call round some time and we can discuss arrangements and talk about _____ _____.

Yours

Christianity in today's world Teacher's Resource Book

© John Murray

Christian Marriage Guide

You have been appointed as the editor of a magazine for young Christians. Your readers are aged 15–20. Many of the letters to your Problem Page are about sex and marriage. You decide that it would be helpful to provide a free pull-out leaflet which gives advice about sex and marriage from a Christian perspective. It is your task to produce that leaflet.

It must be no more than four sides of A5 paper, attractively presented, and should include useful information on the following:

- celebrating and controlling sex

- different ideas about marriage (a sacrament or not?)

- how to prepare for marriage

- some advice from the Bible

- some advice about married life and family life

You will find a lot of information on pages 35–44 of your book.
In selecting advice from the Bible, here are some sources to consider:

Ephesians 5.21–33, respect within marriage

Exodus 20.14, do not commit adultery

Genesis 2.21–25, marriage was part of God's plan

Matthew 5.27–32, Jesus on divorce

Matthew 19.1–9, God hates divorce but allows it because people are 'so hard to teach'

Examination practice: Marriage and divorce

a) i) What is meant by the phrase 'sanctity of marriage'?
ii) Describe what Christianity teaches about the importance of the family. (8)

i) _____

_____

_____

ii) _____

_____

_____

_____

_____

_____

_____

b) Explain the vows which are made during a Christian wedding ceremony. (7)

_____

_____

_____

_____

_____

_____

c) 'If people get divorced they should be allowed to marry someone else in a religious ceremony.'
Do you agree?
Give reasons to support your answer and show that you have thought about different points of view. You
must refer to Christianity in your answer. (5)

_____

_____

_____

_____

_____

_____

MEG (GCSE short course) RE Syllabus B, Paper 2, 1997

Answer guidelines: Marriage and divorce

These are ideas you can use in your answer but remember to make your answers read well as complete sentences.

a) i) Idea of special or set apart. God involved. Marriage is different to just living together.

ii) Family is place of safety, love and commitment. Marriage ceremony says marriage is for: legal sex, bringing up children in security, a covenant of companionship. Family provides for emotional, material and educational needs of all members.

b) In all of circumstances of life:

- faithfulness, fidelity
- joy of bodily union – giving selves to each other
- for all of life, not just till fed up with each other
- whatever happens to them – financial disaster or win the lottery, even if one is seriously ill will stick by each other and cope together, and also enjoy each other's company.

The vows are solemn and binding promises made before God, who will help them to keep them.

c) Arguments for:

- Church must be compassionate
- they must want to be married before God or wouldn't ask
- gives God's seal on second time round
- Church has no right to turn anyone away – would Jesus have done that?
- couple may be Christians who just made mistake or were wronged first time round.

Arguments against:

- vows are for life, makes a mockery if they are not kept
- poor witness to others
- Bible is against remarriage
- how do we know that it means anything to them?

The 'builder's skip'

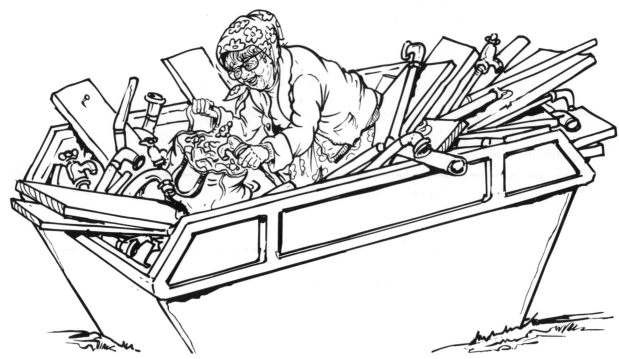

The agnostic writer David Hare made the following comment about the Bible. He said the Bible was like:

> 'a builder's skip, full of old planks and plumbing, waiting to be looted for purely private purposes by any old mad woman with a handbag who happens to come along. No wonder it is the book which has traditionally provided so much inspiration to raving loonies in the street.'

This lively quotation is full of interesting images and needs to be unpacked. Christians may well enjoy Hare's humour but they would be unlikely to agree with his argument.

You could use this quotation to discuss the use of the Bible in relation to any issue.

Try writing an analysis of the quotation in four paragraphs:

Paragraph one

Explain what David Hare means when he makes his comment about the Bible. Key images are:

the builder's skip   *private purposes*   *mad woman/loony*

You will need to make it clear why these key images are included in Hare's argument.

Paragraph two

Explain why Hare thinks that the Bible is inconsistent or open to personal interpretation. Give examples from a topic you have studied of how different Christians use the Bible to support conflicting ideas or beliefs.

Paragraph three

Explain why most Christians would disagree with David Hare. Think about how the Bible is used by Christians and the place it has in Christian tradition. Explain how Christians try to find principles for action in the Bible rather than looking for specific instructions.

Paragraph four

Explain what your overall opinion is. Do you agree with David Hare or not? Explain why you have come to this point of view. Show that you respect the other side of the argument, even if you don't agree with it.

Christian views on homosexuality

One of the skills you need to have for GCSE RE is to be able to make balanced notes. Try your skill with the sources on pages 46–8 of your book, which give different Christian views on homosexuality. Read Sources B, D, E, H, J, K and then make notes as follows:

Some Christians believe that homosexuality is wrong. Evidence I have collected for this point of view includes:

_____

_____

_____

_____

_____

_____

_____

_____

_____

_____

There are other Christians who believe that you can be gay and Christian. Evidence I have collected for this point of view includes:

_____

_____

_____

_____

_____

_____

_____

_____

_____

_____

My personal view is that homosexual love is _____.

I think this because _____

_____

_____

_____

_____

_____

_____

_____

Apartheid, then and now

Use the information on page 50 of your book to complete this letter.

To the Dutch Reformed Church of South Africa

From the Christian Council of Churches in Great Britain

21st June 1986

Dear Sir/Madam,

We are writing to you to express our great concern about what you call the 'Divider' God. We understand you are saying that

_____

_____

_____

If this is true we are surprised to hear such things from fellow Christians. We are, quite frankly, ashamed of your beliefs. We can see no basis for what you are saying in the Bible. In fact, we want you to read again _____

_____

_____

We think it contains an important message for all Churches about the equality of all people in Christ.
We also urge you to read *The Kairos Document* which says

_____

_____

We believe you need to change your views radically and confess your sins now. Support your fellow Christians in South Africa and help bring an end to the terrible apartheid laws in your country!

Yours in Christ,

Prejudice and discrimination

> PREJUDICE is an attitude. It means having an opinion which is not based on fact. For example, 'I think he won't do this job well because he is black.'

> DISCRIMINATION is an action. It means treating someone unfairly because of your prejudice. For example, 'I won't employ him because he is black.'

Cut out the statements at the bottom of this sheet and position them under the table heading you think fits each best. Then add some examples of your own.

Prejudice	Discrimination

'All old people are moody.'	Women were not allowed to vote in this country until 1918.
'Drivers who are women are more likely to cause accidents than men.'	Hitler hated Jews.
In Nazi Germany, Jews were forced to wear yellow badges.	'People over 75 will not be given any priority for hospital beds.'

WORKSHEET 3.13

A *church's anti-racism policy*

This is an outline for your church's anti-racism policy, needed for the Activity on page 53.

1 For part one, **Principles**, write complete sentences – not just notes – which express key Christian ideas of:

- all people's equality before God
- God's love of justice and fairness
- all people to realise their full potential.

2 For part two, **Practical action**, describe practical steps a church could take to eliminate racism. Possible ideas you could consider:

- changes to prayer and worship
- language used
- roles within the church
- social action
- involvement in politics
- dealing with racist incidents.

———— HIGH STREET CHURCH ————

Our anti-racism policy

We are aware that racism affects our church life just as it affects other areas of daily life. This policy sets out principles and practical action for eliminating racism in our church.

Principles

As Christians we believe that:

a) _____

_____

b) _____

_____

c) _____

_____

Practical action

Therefore we promise we will:

a) _____

_____

b) _____

_____

c) _____

_____

---

3 When you have written your policy, discuss: how effective do you think such a policy would be and why?

Christianity in today's world Teacher's Resource Book © John Murray

Does the present treatment of women reflect the mind of Jesus?

This sample essay plan supports the essay-writing task on page 59 of your book. You can write as much as you wish in the gaps and adapt any wording that does not help you.

Christians try to follow the example of Jesus. In my essay I have been asked

to investigate . . .

This is a difficult question to answer because . . .

But it is also an important issue because . . .

There are ways in which discrimination against women is being challenged in

the churches today. In November 1992, women . . . for the first time.

Other people have tried to change the language Christians use . . .

At the same time there is evidence of discrimination against women. For

example . . .

Does this situation reflect the attitude of Jesus to women?

I have studied . . . examples of Jesus meeting with women and I would say

his attitude to women was . . .

One typical example of the way he treated women was . . . which showed . . .

In conclusion I believe that the attitude of the church to women does/does

not reflect the mind of Jesus. My reason for saying this is. . . .

I understand that others might not accept my view.

WORKSHEET 3.15

Examination practice: Prejudice and discrimination

a) Explain, using examples, the difference between prejudice and discrimination. (4)

_____

_____

_____

_____

_____

b) What teaching is given about prejudice and discrimination in the sacred texts of **one** religious tradition? (5)

_____

_____

_____

_____

_____

c) Describe how the teachings you have outlined in part **b)** are put into practice in this tradition with regard to:
i) people of different races **and**
ii) women. (6)

i) _____

_____

_____

_____

ii) _____

_____

_____

_____

d) An Anglican bishop has argued that it is not always wrong to discriminate against other people; it depends on the circumstances.
Do you agree with his view? Give reasons for your opinion, showing that you have thought about more than one point of view. (5)

_____

_____

_____

_____

_____

_____

NEAB (GCSE short course) RE Syllabus D, Paper 2, 1997

Christianity in today's world Teacher's Resource Book © John Murray

WORKSHEET 3.16

Serving others

1 Connect each of the statements to one of the boxes with a line.

It is what Jesus would do if he was here

Visiting someone in prison

Whenever you help someone you are doing that action to Jesus

Feeding the poor

It shows how important God is in your life

Listening to someone's problems

| Reasons to serve others | Ways of serving others |

Giving shelter to the homeless

Caring for the sick

It is our love for God in action

Christians are Jesus' hands, feet and eyes today

Being full of God's love and joy for people

2 Match up the sentences in the first table below with the correct example in the second table.

Decision
a) how to vote at an election
b) deciding what job to do
c) whether to marry and how to raise a family
d) what to buy in shops
e) what organisations to give money or time to

How it might allow a Christian to serve others
i) by making sure I buy brands that have been fairly traded
ii) by voting for someone who will try and help the poor
iii) by supporting charities such as Christian Aid which help people on my behalf in the developing world
iv) to make serving others a fun part of family life
v) I will use my strengths and talents to do a job where I can help people and bring in more of God's values in the workplace

WORKSHEET 3.17

Respect for authority

Fill in these 'think bubbles'. You could get some ideas from Source E on page 61.

Someone I might
obey:

Someone I might
respect:

Someone I might see
as an authority figure:

Then complete:

I might obey this person/these people because: _____

_____

I might respect this person/these people because: _____

_____

I might see this person/these people as authority figures because: _____

_____

Christianity in today's world Teacher's Resource Book   © John Murray

WORKSHEET 3.18

Examination practice: The individual in society

a) Choose **one** religious tradition you have studied. What does it teach about respecting the authority of the state and its laws? (5)

_____

_____

_____

_____

_____

_____

b) How might
   i) an individual believer, **and**
   ii) a religious community as a whole
show respect for the authority of the state? (4)

   i) _____

      _____

      _____

   ii) _____

      _____

      _____

c) From time to time a person's religion can come into conflict with the authority of the state. Describe briefly **one** such occasion and explain a religious believer's response to such a conflict. (6)

_____

_____

_____

_____

_____

_____

_____

d) 'Religious believers have more responsibility than others to protest against unjust laws.' Do you agree? Give reasons for your opinion, showing that you have thought about more than one point of view. (5)

_____

_____

_____

_____

_____

_____

_____

_____

NEAB (GCSE short course) RE Syllabus D, Paper 2, 1997

WORKSHEET 3.19

Bible file cards: Relationships

RELATIONSHIPS

Reference: 1 Corinthians 6.15–17

Context: NT – Paul

Summary: The Christian's body is the Temple of the Holy Spirit

Application: Do not abuse body in sex or other ways

RELATIONSHIPS

Reference: Exodus 20.14

Context: OT – one of Ten Commandments

Summary: Do not commit adultery

Application: Specialness of sex in marriage

RELATIONSHIPS

Reference: Ephesians 5.21–33

Context: NT – Paul

Summary: Husbands love wives, wives submit to husbands, both submit to each other

Application: Complementary roles in marriage

RELATIONSHIPS

Reference: Matthew 19.3–9

Context: NT – Jesus

Summary: Pharisees ask why Moses allows divorce, Jesus says because people are 'so hard to teach' – would make life difficult for each other

Application: Teaching on divorce

RELATIONSHIPS

Reference: Romans 13.1–7

Context: NT – Paul

Summary: Submit to earthly authority – put there by God

Application: Obey authorities

RELATIONSHIPS

Reference: John 15.12

Context: NT – Jesus

Summary: 'Love one another as I have loved you'

Application: Jesus loved all equally, so should we

RELATIONSHIPS

Reference: Galatians 3.28

Context: NT – Paul

Summary: There is not Jew or Gentile, slave or free, man or woman, all are one in JC

Application: Equality of all people in Christian faith

RELATIONSHIPS

Reference: Romans 1.26–7

Context: NT – Paul

Summary: Condemns homosexual practices

Application: Attitudes to homosexuality

RELATIONSHIPS

Reference: Matthew 25.31–46

Context: NT – Jesus (parable)

Summary: King will divide people at end of world – those who cared for poor, sick and needy will go to Heaven, rest will not; 'doing this is doing it for God'

Application: Service, aid to Third World

RELATIONSHIPS

Reference: Luke 10.25–37

Context: NT – Jesus (parable)

Summary: Good Samaritan: man beaten up and left for dead, ignored by two of own people, enemy comes by and cares for him; 'you go and do same'

Application: Prejudice, care for all

End of Unit Quiz: Relationships

Test yourself or your neighbour with this quick quiz.

1 Define the word *marriage*.

2 When people say that marriage is a *covenant*, what do they mean?

3 State two arguments that Christians might use for not having sex before you are married.

4 Write out one Bible passage that might be used by Christians to show that how they treat their bodies matters.

5 Give two reasons for Christians to get married.

6 What does 'Do not commit adultery' mean?

7 Explain two things that the ring symbolises at a Christian wedding.

8 Why do Roman Catholic Christians believe that marriage is a sacrament?

9 Give two causes of difficulties in a marriage.

10 Why do some Christians believe divorce can be God's will?

11 State one thing Jesus said about divorce.

12 Give one reason why some Christians believe it is morally wrong to be a practising homosexual.

13 Give one reason why some Christians believe that to be a practising homosexual can be moral.

14 Write out one Church view on homosexuality.

15 Define *racism*.

16 What does the Commission for Racial Equality do?

17 Write out one Bible passage that could be used by Christians against racism.

18 If you use someone as a 'scapegoat' what do you do to them?

19 What is *genocide*? Give an example from history.

20 State one way in which the Church works against racism.

21 Define *sexism*.

22 Give an example of gender prejudice.

23 Give an example of gender discrimination. (Remember that prejudice and discrimination are different.)

24 Explain why some Christians have felt that the Church is sexist.

25 State two arguments for women having equal rights to those of men in society.

Word list: Relationships

You need to know all of these words and their meanings.

Sex, marriage and divorce

Adultery   A sexual relationship with someone other than the marriage partner

Agape   Christian love

Celibate   Choosing not to have a sexual partner, for religious reasons

Commitment   Sticking by someone

Contract   Legally binding agreement

Covenant   Agreement, contract

Fidelity   Faithfulness to your marriage partner

Fornication   Sex before marriage, or outside marriage

Friendship   A trusting relationship between two or more people

Heterosexual   One who chooses a partner of the opposite sex

Homosexual   One who chooses a partner of the same sex

Marriage   A legal agreement between a man and a woman to share their lives together

Monogamy   Having one marriage partner

Permissive   Accepting or following an immoral lifestyle

Polygamy   Having more than one marriage partner

Promiscuity   Having many sexual relationships

Reconciliation   To sort out problems and get back together as friends/partners

Prejudice and discrimination

Anti-Semitism   Hatred of Jews, leading to action against them

Apartheid   A policy of racial separation which formerly operated in South Africa

Civil Rights   The rights of being treated equally in society, e.g. all people having the right to vote

Commission for Racial Equality (CRE)   An organisation which helps races mix

Democracy   People having equal rights and choosing how to govern themselves

Dictatorship   One person ruling and telling others what to do

Discrimination   An action treating someone unfairly

Free speech   Being able to say what you like in public

Gentile   Non-Jew

Genocide   The destruction of a whole race of people

Ghetto   Area of (often poor) housing where people of similar 'type' live

Immigration   People coming to live in one country from another

Integration   Mixing of races in areas of life

Justice   Fair treatment

Ku Klux Klan   A sinister, racist white group in the USA

National Front   A political organisation which aims to 'repatriate' coloured people

Nationalist   Being very loyal to one's country

Prejudice   A thought that makes a judgement about someone without any evidence

Race relations   How well different races get on together

Races   Subdivisions of mankind, based on physical characteristics

Racist   Believing that a particular race (your own) is superior

Scapegoat   Using one person to take the blame for something

Segregation   Keeping races apart

Sexism   Being prejudiced against someone because of their gender; nearly always used of prejudice against women

UNIT 4
Global issues

Overview

An introduction (4.1) draws out the link between individual action and global impact in an ever-smaller world. The unit then investigates three issues: wealth and poverty (4.2), the environment (4.3) and war and peace (4.4). The compulsory topic for NEAB Syllabus D is wealth and poverty, although this may change with time.

Most GCSE students will have a natural interest in these topics and may well feel deeply about issues such as the environment. There are also rich resources to be found in the print and TV media almost every day, and the organisations listed on pages 13–14 will be keen to send you information. These topics should therefore be popular.

However, remember that investigation of the topics needs to go beyond the rather clichéd treatment characteristic of some media coverage, so that there can be realistic discussion and balanced judgements can be reached. Remember too that this is RE – it is students' understanding of the religious perspective on such issues that is the main focus of this course and that will interest the examiners.

Starting strategies

Page 65

The unit starts in the same way as others, with a full-page visual to provoke discussion of the issues. This is reproduced with questions on **Worksheet 4.1**. Use this as a basis for class discussion. How do the students feel about world issues? Are they just too overwhelming? What can we do?

4.1 How can individuals change the world?

The introductory discussion leads naturally on to page 66 where the ideas are teased out as a more structured activity.

Page 66

SOURCE A This is worth discussion in its own right. It is important to help students to see that Christians do not all rush out to hand over all of their savings to the latest charity to hit the headlines. Nor can they all leave home and family to go and work in a Third World country or to help the needy in other ways. Christians may need to do something, but it may not be spectacular. When asked what they can do about a global issue a Christian may well respond that all they can do is to pray. This is also a perfectly justifiable examination answer, if it is clearly explained.

4.2 How should Christians use their money?

Some of the richest people in the world would call themselves Christians. Some of the poorest, too. Some Christians feel that great personal wealth is incompatible with Christian values. Others feel that wealth is a sign of God's blessing on them – their riches are a gift from God. Both extremes can find support in the Bible. The challenge for the teacher tackling this topic is therefore how to do justice to the different views *and* help students to come to their own view?

This challenge dictates the approach of the issue raiser (page 67) and the contrasting case studies of John Templeton and the Iona Community (pages 68–9). These are followed by a case study of Christian Aid (pages 70–72), which meets the NEAB Syllabus D specific requirement that candidates should study 'a religious organisation which alleviates poverty' while also providing an investigation of the issues of wealth and poverty on the global scale.

A number of videos exist which may also be helpful. The BBC series *Taking Issue* has a programme on *Wealth and Poverty*, and the series *Christianity in a Changing World* has one on *Materialism*.

It is also worth keeping an eye open for good documentaries on Third World issues or poverty in this country to use as starters for discussions.

We have focused on Christian Aid but teachers could consider the work of other organisations, such as CAFOD or Tear Fund, alongside or instead of Christian Aid if students were particularly interested, or if you have a contact with another organisation.

Page 67
SOURCE A Keep a record of students' responses to the questions since the issue is returned to in the 'Save As' activity on page 73.

Pages 68–9
Should Christians be rich?

Although John Templeton and the Iona Community represent opposite ends of the spectrum in terms of their attitudes towards wealth, it is important to stress throughout that they nevertheless have a mutual respect for each other's work which is demonstrated in the giving and receiving of the Templeton award (see Focus Task, page 69).

To develop this spread further you could run a role play in which John Templeton meets George MacLeod, founder of the Iona Community. Their starter statements could be the ones in word bubbles at the top of the spread. How would the conversations develop from there?

Page 69

Question 7 This issue is returned to in investigating responses to Christian Aid Week (page 72).

Worksheet 4.2 is a homework sheet that investigates changing views of which possessions are luxuries, which are necessities. Which are considered the bare essential items? This could alternatively be used with page 72.

Pages 70–72

How does Christian Aid fight poverty?

The information on pages 70–71 is quite concise. For a more sustained investigation, interested students could write to Christian Aid for more information about their work. A short video is available from them (for which a small donation is suggested) showing examples of other work they do.

Worksheet 4.3 supports this spread – students annotate and explain a copy of Source H.

Page 71

Questions 1 and 2 Another topical Christian Aid campaign is that for the working conditions of workers making trainers and footballs for sale to richer nations.

Page 72

ACTIVITY A The issue about priorities for giving is worth further development. Here are some arguments on both sides for students to consider:

- Some Third World countries have little or no social security – we have.
- Jesus did not specify where to give, just that we give.
- The need is far greater in other countries.
- It's our money to give as we like.
- Some people are more generous if they know it is going to be spent overseas.
- Others are less generous if they know that!
- The Church is not setting a very good example if it does not care for the poor in this land.
- The number of poor people here is growing – we must do something about it quickly.

ACTIVITY B The photos will lead to discussion of spending on church buildings. The same question could be asked at the individual level (see Worksheet 4.2).

Page 73

Poverty or inequality?

FOCUS TASK Worksheet 4.3 could be used to support task 3. In task 4, the windows could be designed in pairs: problem/action. For task 5, give students some structure for their guidelines if necessary, e.g.

- how much to give away
- who to give to
- how to invest
- what to spend on self and on others
- what churches are to spend on themselves.

4.3 Responsible stewards or plundering idiots?

Often books on religion and the environment concentrate on problems and negative issues. We have tried a different tack by beginning with Christians celebrating the environment using a Derbyshire well-dressing festival (pages 74–5) as the issue raiser. Pages 76–7 then investigate the way Christians' ideas about Creation give them both rights and responsibilities for the environment.

Christians who are aware of their responsibility for the environment need to call their own behaviour and that of others to account. Pages 78–9 investigate how three denominations and one individual have done and are doing this.

Finally, pages 80–81 provide a self-contained investigation on the specific issue of animal rights which features in a number of syllabuses.

Environmental issues lend themselves to cross-curricular activities. Links could be made with the Art Department; trips could be organised in conjunction with Science, Geography, PSE or Humanities teachers as an excellent opportunity to develop SMSC themes across the curriculum. Veronica Williams' book on *Beliefs, Values and the Environment* (published by CEM) is useful in this respect.

Songs of Praise or other such religious TV programmes, especially at Harvest time, are also useful starters with the question asked: is this reality?

Page 75

ACTIVITIES A AND B These are demanding and open-ended tasks. You could scale them down considerably for some students, e.g. in A by simply asking them to design their own well-dressing picture. You could specify a theme for some students or leave them to choose their own if you think they can do so. You could provide a template for them to work with.

Page 76

The Christian belief in God's gift of Creation

SOURCE C This could lead to creative work. Students could go out and observe the dappling effect that Hopkins talks about – in woodland in sunlight, or on water, or on animals. They could write down their own thoughts and feelings about what they are watching, or they could photograph the dappling effects. They could then use these thoughts and images to inspire their own poetry or visual artwork based on what they have seen.

Question 1 The idea of this question is to explore whether this hymn gets the balance right. You could suggest a statement for students to disagree or agree with, e.g. 'This children's hymn is far too sentimental. The world is not like that. Children should not be encouraged to sing it.'

Other popular hymns could be examined in this way, particularly Harvest Festival hymns. You could also look at more modern hymns on similar topics to see if they take a different approach.

However, if your students (or you yourself) are particularly critical of existing hymns you ought also to have a go at doing better yourself! Try writing another, more realistic verse (to the same tune or a new one).

Page 77

Question 3 One key idea in stewardship of the environment is that every little helps, although a good discussion should ensue as to whether some aspects of stewardship are more significant than others and why.

Worksheet 4.4 pursues this idea, further testing out 'How green are you?' through a multiple-choice quiz which examines the environmental impact of the students' own lifestyle.

Page 78

The response to environmental issues by Christian denominations

FOCUS TASK Some students may need support for this. **Worksheet 4.5** provides support for task 1 by pre-selecting the 'teaching points' for students; they then simply look for evidence of each in Sources G–I.

Worksheet 4.6 supports task 2 and provides a 'pledge form' to structure students' answers.

Pages 80–81

Animal rights versus human rights

SOURCE L Worksheet 4.7 examines the idea of pet services. It is ideal for homework – students design their own animal service.

Worksheet 4.8 provides examination practice on environmental issues.

4.4 Is it ever right to fight?

A single image (page 82) is used as the issue raiser, leading into three pages (83–5) explaining the three key ideas of **holy war**, **just war** and **pacifism** (no war). This may be all that students need to cover for some syllabuses.

Pages 86 is extension material on the arms trade; page 87 is extension material on violence in the struggle for liberation, which builds on the work on Liberation Theology started on page 62.

Page 82

ACTIVITY The painting is called *In the Image of Man*. It was painted just after the Second World War (which students should have studied in their Key Stage 3 History course). The picture shows the damage that war can do to society, but also the damage it can do religion.

Investigating the ways in which this may be true will be a rich starting point for the topic of war and peace.

DISCUSS The quotation is from a 15-year-old student, who came out with it in a class debate.

Pages 83–5

What do Christians believe about war?

SAVE AS . . . Before students annotate their own copy you could do a large version on OHT or the board and talk them through the content of pages 83–5.

Page 84

SOURCE C Students may need to memorise these criteria for their examination.

Question 1 This will not be easy for any students who have not studied the Second World War. **Worksheet 4.9** supports the task. There is a second worksheet providing an alternative, based on the Gulf War of 1991.

SOURCE E It is worth focusing some class discussion on this famous image.

Page 85

FOCUS TASK You could stimulate ideas for task 3 with a collection of images from books or magazines which give different ideas about peace. The students could prioritise them or add to them.

We have not gone into detail on nuclear war in the Student's Book, but **Worksheet 4.10** teases out the controversy about unilateral nuclear disarmament. It can be used as a homework sheet or a debate starter.

Page 87

Violence v. non-violence in the struggle for liberation

Pages 62–3 on Liberation Theology provide important background to this page.

FOCUS TASK These are review questions for the entire investigation and therefore cover similar ground to some of the tasks on pages 83–5.

Worksheet 4.11 provides examination practice on war and peace, together with the examiner's mark scheme to guide students in developing their answers.

Page 88

Global issues – Review task

This is supported by various other review and revision tasks: **Worksheet 4.12** sets up a 'Just a Minute' session based on various themes from the unit; **Worksheet 4.13** provides Bible file cards on key passages related to the global issues covered in this unit which students might need to be aware of for their examination; **Worksheet 4.14** is an end of unit test; **Worksheet 4.15** is a word list.

WORKSHEET 4.1

Global issues

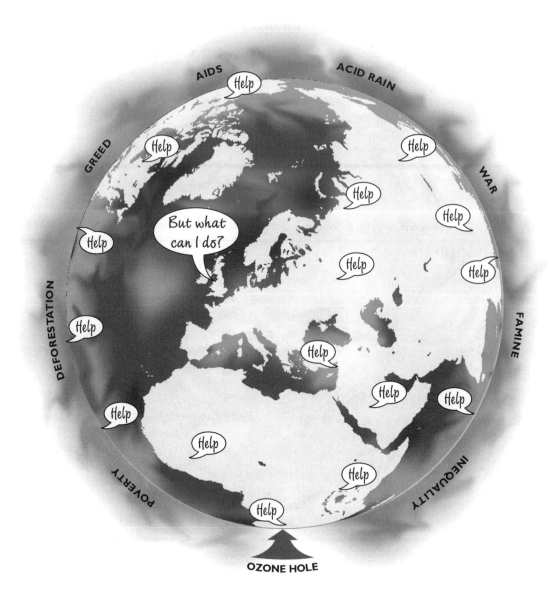

1 Highlight on this illustration any global issues that are really important to you.
2 Add any that you think are missing. You can use words or pictures.
3 For one issue you have highlighted write about:
   a) how people might feel overwhelmed by the issue

_____

_____

_____

   b) one simple way in which people might take positive action.

_____

_____

_____

4 Compare your ideas with a partner's.

Christianity in today's world Teacher's Resource Book   © John Murray

Priorities

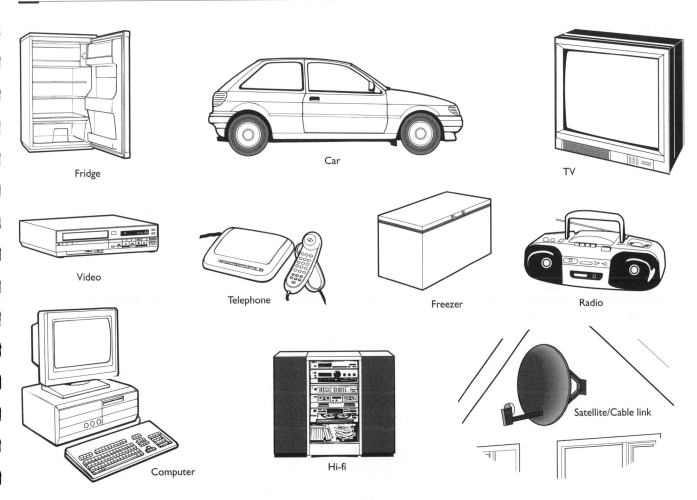

Fridge

Car

TV

Video

Telephone

Freezer

Radio

Computer

Hi-fi

Satellite/Cable link

Many people in Britain would consider themselves poor if they didn't have these things. Yet only 40 years ago ordinary people in Britain would have lived happy lives with none of them.

> I haven't had a television since my last one was stolen. Some people think I'm weird; others seem quite impressed. I don't miss it. I go out with my friends instead. We go around to each others' houses, chat, listen to music, go to the cinema. If I stay in I listen to the radio or read books and magazines.

> We didn't have a fridge in our house until I was seven or eight. It didn't matter. We just shopped differently, every few days getting what we needed. I remember the fridge arriving. We came back on the train from a holiday in Wales. The fridge was just there: it was a Hotpoint Iced Diamond!

1 Decide whether you could or could not live without each of the items illustrated.
   Explain the reasons for your choice.
2 If you could have just two, which would you choose? Which could you most easily do without?
   See if you can agree with a partner the two most essential and the two least essential items.
3 Try to work out with your partner what priorities you share, and what the differences are.

How Christian Aid helps

1 Re-read the information about the work of Christian Aid on pages 70–71 of your book.

2 Add notes around this diagram to explain each area of Christian Aid's work. You can add examples (from pages 70–71) of Christian Aid's development work, campaigning and fundraising. You can add examples of emergency relief from events which have been in the news.

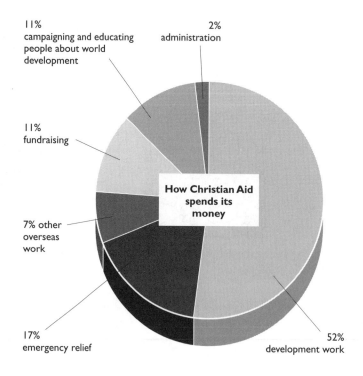

11%
campaigning and educating
people about world
development

2%
administration

11%
fundraising

7% other
overseas
work

**How Christian Aid
spends its
money**

17%
emergency relief

52%
development work

3 Write here the slogan of Christian Aid and explain what it means. If you have difficulty you can refer to page 126 of your book.

_____

_____

_____

4 Do you think Christian Aid spend their money in the right way? Write a sentence to explain your view.

_____

_____

How green are you?

Find out how environmentally aware you are with this quiz. Answer honestly and then look up your scores to find out how much you care about the Earth.

HOW GREEN ARE YOU?

1 What sort of deodorant do you buy?
- **a)** Roll-on, it's ozone friendly.
- **b)** Spray-on, it's easy to use.
- **c)** I don't know, my Mum buys it for me.
- **d)** What's deodorant?

2 What do you do with your used envelopes?
- **a)** Re-use them as envelopes with those little labels you can get.
- **b)** Use them to file things in.
- **c)** Throw them in a bin.
- **d)** Make paper aeroplanes.

3 You are out shopping and a member of Greenpeace asks you to join up. How do you react?
- **a)** I'm already a member.
- **b)** What a good idea, I'll join.
- **c)** Sign up, but under a false name.
- **d)** Rush away pretending to be in a hurry.

4 Would you buy a snakeskin bag or a tortoiseshell item?
- **a)** No, it's cruel to the animals.
- **b)** No, it's not necessary.
- **c)** Only if it was a gift for someone else.
- **d)** Of course, I only buy the best.

5 Do you look for 'not tested on animals' labels on make-up and toiletries?
- **a)** Always, I'd hate to think that animals suffered for my vanity.
- **b)** Yes, if I remember.
- **c)** Yes, because I'm a bit suspicious, what if they are not safe for humans?
- **d)** Who cares about Fido, people come first.

6 What do you do with used soft drink cans?
- **a)** Take them to one of those can banks which collects for charity.
- **b)** Get some ideas from *Blue Peter* or *Art Attack* and make them into interesting things.
- **c)** Put them in a bin.
- **d)** Crunch them in my fist to impress my friends, then I think I drop them on the floor.

7 Would you join the campaign to save whales?
- **a)** Yes, they are a vital part of the ecological system of the sea.
- **b)** Yes, they are beautiful creatures.
- **c)** Not sure, they can be dangerous can't they?
- **d)** Wales is such a small country, does it really matter?

8 Would you pay more to buy organic vegetables?
- **a)** Yes, the way they're produced is much better for the environment.
- **b)** No, I'd grow my own instead.
- **c)** Yes, they're better for you and they taste better.
- **d)** Are they more expensive? My Mum does the shopping so I leave all that to her.

9 What do you feel about the destruction of the rainforests?
- **a)** It's destroying the careful balance of nature.
- **b)** It is awful that people who live there are losing their livelihoods.
- **c)** It's rather a long way away.
- **d)** It still seems to rain a lot where I live.

10 Would you buy your Mum a fur coat if you won the pools?
- **a)** No, I'd give a lot of money to an animal charity.
- **b)** No, I'd pay for a safari to Africa to see wildlife at its best.
- **c)** Yes, she has cared for me and she deserves the best.
- **d)** No, you can't be sure it's dead.

Scores:

Mostly a's: You really seem to care about the environment in which you live and always put creation first before your own comfort. Well done!

Mostly b's: You do care about the environment, although there are times when perhaps you are not as well informed as you might be. Try getting hold of some reading matter about these issues.

Mostly c's: You certainly care about people and about doing your best, although often you seem a little misguided and tend to do the wrong thing in the long run. Try to think about what really matters and not just superficial things.

Mostly d's: Well you really are a drain on the Earth's resources aren't you! You either don't care or won't learn. Why not find out a bit more about these important matters? Otherwise you may find that the things you take for granted one day are no longer there for you.

WORKSHEET 4.5

Christian teaching on the environment

Look for evidence of each Christian teaching point in Sources G to I on page 78.
When you find it tick the relevant box in the next three columns and include a
relevant quotation from the source.

Christian teaching on the environment	Catholic (Source G)	Anglican (Source H)	Methodist (Source I)
God created the world			
People are responsible for looking after it			
There is great beauty in the natural world			
Humans are created in the image of God			
Creation is a gift from God			
The world should be just and peaceful			

Christianity in today's world Teacher's Resource Book

A *Christian pledge on the environment*

Use this worksheet for question 2 in Focus Task A, page 78.

1 Choose one of the statements: Catholic (Source G), Anglican (Source H) or Methodist (Source I).
2 Choose one or two important sentences from it to focus on.
3 Work out measures that your denomination could take to apply their beliefs.
4 Complete this pledge form to record your answer.

Our Pledge

from _____

In our statement _____

_____

_____

we stated our belief that _____

_____

_____

Therefore we intend to take the following steps to improve our environment:

1 _____

_____

2 _____

_____

3 _____

_____

Then we will celebrate our achievement by _____

_____

_____

If we do not meet these targets we will _____

_____

_____

Pet service

Some churches hold annual 'pet services' or 'animal services' to which people (especially children) are invited to bring their animals to give thanks to God for the joy that they bring, and to ask for God's blessing on them.

One recent edition of the BBC religious programme *Songs of Praise* was broadcast from the Wood Green Animal Shelter in Huntingdon. Hundreds of people turned up with many different sorts of animals to sing God's praise. The programme featured people who, as Christians, worked with animals, either as their job (for example an RSPCA officer who was seen catching a swan which had swallowed lead shot and then releasing it back to the wild) or in their leisure time (a lady was interviewed about the riding group she ran for disabled people, believing that the horses helped to 'bring out' people with learning difficulties).

Ely Cathedral holds an annual pet service for the Wood Green Animal Shelter which is very popular with local people (though perhaps not with the cathedral's cleaners!). Canon Green of the cathedral explained:

> The cathedral gives room to the service because we believe animals are a part of Creation – they bring so much pleasure to many people and they display a sense of loyalty sadly lacking in many human relationships.

1 Devise an order of service for a pet service. You could include relevant hymns, Bible readings, prayers or other items. Try to include both positive and negative aspects of humans' treatment and use of animals. You could have thanksgiving for animals, confession for cruelty to animals and intercession to God on behalf of animals.

2 Discuss: why do you think that some Christians might disapprove of such services?

PET SERVICE
Order of Service

WORKSHEET 4.8

Examination practice: Environmental issues

a) i) What is meant by 'stewardship'?
ii) Describe Christian teaching about how people should care for the environment. (8)

i) _____

_____

ii) _____

_____

_____

_____

_____

_____

_____

b) Explain why some Christians feel that they should not eat meat. (7)

_____

_____

_____

_____

_____

_____

c) 'We cannot really love God if we do not take care of the world we live in and the things that live in it.'
Do you agree?
Give reasons to support your answer and show that you have thought about different points of view. You must refer to Christianity in your answer. (5)

_____

_____

_____

_____

_____

_____

MEG (GCSE short course) RE Syllabus B, Paper 2, 1997

WORKSHEET 4.9

Was the Second World War a just war?

Tests for a just war	Britain's war against Hitler's Germany in the Second World War	Just war? ✔ or ✘ or ? and explanation
1. War started and controlled by authority of state.	War was declared and controlled by the democratically elected British Government.	
2. Those attacked deserve it – just cause.	Hitler had already invaded or taken over two neighbouring countries in his attempts to gain more territory for Germany.	
3. War fought to promote good and avoid evil – just intention.	The war was declared to prevent Hitler from invading other areas.	
4. War is last resort, other ways of solving conflict have been tried.	For four years previously there had been tense negotiations to try to settle the problem without a war. The British had allowed Hitler to get his own way to avoid a war.	
5. Innocent civilians should not be killed, proportionality – only the necessary force or weapons should be used.	There was intense bombing of German cities by British bombers. Hundreds of thousands of German civilians were killed.	
6. Peace must be resumed at the end of the conflict.	Germany was totally defeated and peace was re-established between Britain and Germany. Today they are close allies.	

Christianity in today's world Teacher's Resource Book

Was the Gulf War a just war?

This conflict took place in the Middle East in early 1991. On 2nd August 1990 Iraq had invaded Kuwait (a smaller country but rich in oilfields). After trying alternative sanctions, a coalition of United Nations (UN) forces attacked Iraq (and Kuwait) on 16th January 1991. Iraq eventually withdrew from Kuwait on 3rd March.

1 Read the first column of the table (on the next sheet), which lists the conditions of a just war.
2 Cut out the following six statements about the Gulf War.
3 Paste them in the correct place in the second column of the table.
4 Fill in the third column to say whether you think each action was just or not and explain your view.

The UN imposed sanctions against Iraq and demanded a withdrawal from Kuwait by 15th January 1991.

Thousands of Iraqi and Kuwaiti victims were killed or injured, many of them civilians. The UN used laser-guided bombs and long-range missiles as well as conventional weapons; Iraq used chemical weapons and long-range missiles.

The UN declared war, with each member of the defence force being backed by their own government.

The UN was defending the small, oil-rich, country of Kuwait.

It was felt necessary to defeat the dictatorship of Saddam Hussein in Iraq.

A permanent cease-fire was agreed on 6th April, but Iraq still has stockpiles of chemical and biological weapons.

Was the Gulf War a just war?

Tests for a just war	The war against Iraq in the Gulf War	Just war? ✔ or ✗ or ? and explanation
1. War started and controlled by authority of state.		
2. Those attacked deserve it – just cause.		
3. War fought to promote good and avoid evil – just intention.		
4. War is last resort, other ways of solving conflict have been tried.		
5. Innocent civilians should not be killed, proportionality – only the necessary force or weapons should be used.		
6. Peace must be resumed at the end of the conflict.		

Unilateral nuclear disarmament

Some people today believe that if there were another world war it would be a
nuclear war and that the world as we know it would be destroyed. Many
Christians support nuclear disarmament. However they would disagree about
how to achieve this. Most would hope for **multilateral** disarmament – all
countries (or several) disarming together by agreement. Others think this is
impossible to achieve and they call for **unilateral** disarmament – for their own
country to take a lead and disarm, whatever the others do.

Here are some arguments for and against unilateral nuclear disarmament.
Match each argument with its opposite.

For unilateral disarmament	Against unilateral disarmament
1 Nuclear war would result in mass destruction of the whole world today. That is evil in itself. We must destroy the weapons.	A We always need a deterrent – who can tell what the future holds?
2 We no longer need a deterrent (the cold war is over) and to keep weapons for this end is wrong – we may use them simply because we have them.	B What is the point of having good education and health care if you have no country to enjoy them because of war?
3 By having nuclear weapons we make ourselves a vulnerable target.	C Use of nuclear weapons in error is practically impossible these days because of careful checks.
4 One country should set an example.	D It is not loving your neighbour not to protect him.
5 The vast sums of money being spent on weapons and defence could be used on positive things like education and health care.	E By having nuclear weapons we have power – the enemy would not strike us as we would retaliate and they could not win.
6 There could be a mistake and the weapons used in error.	F Even if we destroyed our weapons, others would not necessarily follow – that is not reality.
7 If we do not have the weapons we make nuclear war less likely.	G It is impossible to 'disinvent' these weapons. They are a fact of life.
8 It is not loving your neighbour to destroy him with nuclear weapons.	H Other countries (some ruled by evil dictators) could still have the weapons, we do not prevent war alone.

WORKSHEET 4.11

Examination practice: War and peace

This takes a different approach from earlier examination practice sheets. You have an examiner's mark scheme to discuss in class before you start and to help you write your answer to each question.

a) What is meant by the terms 'holy war' and 'just war'? (4)

Answer guidelines and mark scheme
Holy war = war which is fought to defend a faith/religion; a war which is believed to be the will of God. (2 marks)
Just war = war which follows the principles of a 'just war', e.g. proper authority/lawful government/just cause/right a wrong/stop injustice/defend against attack/last resort/proportionate methods/civilians protected/limited force/reasonable chance of victory/otherwise war is a waste of life and resources/good gained by victory greater than evil which led to war. (2 marks for 2 of the above)

b) Choose **one** twentieth century war and explain whether you think it was a 'holy war', a 'just war' or neither. Give reasons to support your opinion. (6)

Answer guidelines and mark scheme
Any 20th century war can be chosen. The 6 marks here for evaluation will be given for justifying the opinion. In each case you must show that the chosen example fulfils the conditions of either a holy war or a just war. In the case of 'neither', you must show by giving examples why the war chosen does not fulfil the conditions of either.
1–2 marks = identification of 20th century war and opinion stated that it was just or holy or neither with one reason to support opinion.
3 marks = opinion + one reason supported by two examples.
4 marks = opinion + two reasons with examples to support each.
5–6 marks = opinion + two or more reasons with examples well-supported by argument or evidence.

c) Explain why some religious believers take part in war and others refuse to do so. (10)

Answer guidelines and mark scheme
Two contrasting attitudes/beliefs required from within any religious tradition, one of which accepts war and one of which rejects war, e.g. Christian pacifism, Quakers' position, outlined – nothing justifies taking human life/co-operation is better than conflict. Examples of Jesus' teaching and non-violent behaviour, e.g. arrest of Jesus (Matthew 26.47–53), love your enemies (Matthew 5.43–48), teaching about an eye for an eye (Matthew 5.38–42). Inconsistent with Christian principles of brotherhood of man/sanctity of life. Moral arguments as to the futility/dangers of war in settling disputes. Civilian casualties/destruction of environment/great suffering/impossibility of nuclear 'just war'.
5 marks will be given for each side of the argument broken down as follows:
1 mark = simple statement of one reason.
2 marks = one reason developed or elaborated, or two reasons simply stated.
3 marks = two reasons, one of which may be developed.
4 marks = two reasons developed or elaborated, or three reasons simply stated.
5 marks = clear understanding shown by good development of three or more appropriate reasons.

NEAB (GCSE short course) RE Syllabus D, Specimen Paper 2

Christianity in today's world Teacher's Resource Book © John Murray

WORKSHEET 4.12

Just a Minute: Global issues

Note to teachers:
1 Copy and cut out the statements on this sheet.
2 Give each student one of the statements.
3 Ask the students to prepare notes which will enable them to speak in support of their statement for at least one minute, with no pauses! They should try to include relevant Christian teachings or ideas too. If they disagree with the statement it should not matter – they can put their own views afterwards.

1 It is a sin for Christians to be rich.	2 It is a sin for Christians to be rich and not to share their wealth.	3 'The love of money is the root of all evil.' (St. Paul)
4 The Bible teaches that Christians should care for the poor.	5 The Iona Community is a good example of being poor in Jesus' name.	6 Reasons why people support the work of Christian Aid.
7 Christians should get involved in politics.	8 Christians should only give to religious charities.	9 Well-dressing is not a Christian festival.
10 Christians should care for the world.	11 It is not just Christians who should care for God's world.	12 Ways of being a good steward of the Earth's resources.
13 The environment is being damaged by the selfishness of humans.	14 Animals have as much right to respect as humans.	15 Humans are always more important than animals.
16 Christians should never fight.	17 A just war is not possible today.	18 Despite modern warfare, it is still possible to have a just war
19 Pacifism is for cowards.	20 It is not possible to be a pacifist today.	

WORKSHEET 4.13

Bible file cards: Global issues

Reference: Luke 12.13–21

GLOBAL ISSUES

Context: NT – Jesus (parable)

Summary: The Rich Fool: man has lots of crops, tears down old barns to build bigger ones and store for winter. God says he will die and who will get his wealth?

Application: Selfishness, waste

Reference: Mark 11.15–18

GLOBAL ISSUES

Context: NT – Gospel

Summary: Jesus enters the Temple just before his death and throws out the traders in a fury

Application: Wrong to commercialise religion and make money from it

---

Reference: Luke 16.19–31

GLOBAL ISSUES

Context: NT – Jesus (parable)

Summary: Lazarus – poor man – dies and goes to Heaven; rich man dies and goes to Hell, wants Lazarus to help him but it's too late

Application: Caring for the poor

Reference: Matthew 6.19–21

GLOBAL ISSUES

Context: NT – Jesus (Sermon on Mount)

Summary: Do not store up treasure on Earth

Application: Sharing wealth

Reference: Acts 4.32–7

GLOBAL ISSUES

Context: NT, early Church

Summary: The first Christians shared their possessions and sold what they did not need, giving money to poor

Application: Early example of Christian Aid

Reference: James 2.4–17

GLOBAL ISSUES

Context: NT – James

Summary: Faith without actions is useless

Application: Need for Christians to care and share

Reference: Psalm 8

GLOBAL ISSUES

Context: OT – Psalmist

Summary: How great God's Creation is and how puny and mortal human beings are in comparison

Application: Greatness of Creation

Reference: Genesis 1 and 2

GLOBAL ISSUES

Context: OT – Creation stories

Summary: Humans given responsibility to care for Creation

Application: Responsibility for the environment

Reference: Matthew 5.9

GLOBAL ISSUES

Context: NT – Jesus (Sermon on Mount)

Summary: Blessed are the peacemakers (a beatitude)

Application: Pacifism

Reference: Matthew 26.47–53

GLOBAL ISSUES

Context: NT – Gospel

Summary: Jesus is arrested and his disciples take out weapons to defend selves. Jesus rebukes them: 'He who lives by the sword will die by the sword'

Application: Christian opposition to violence

Christianity in today's world Teacher's Resource Book © John Murray

End of Unit Quiz: Global issues

Test yourself or your neighbour with this quick quiz.

1 State two global problems.

2 What is money?

3 What is materialism?

4 What does Jesus teach about wealth in the Sermon on the Mount?

5 How did the first Christians show that they were good stewards of their wealth?

6 For what is Sir John Templeton famous?

7 What is the Iona Community?

8 List four aspects of the work of Christian Aid.

9 What are long-term and short-term aid?

10 Give one reason why Christians should be involved in politics in the Third World.

11 Give one reason why they should not.

12 What do Christians mean when they talk about the spiritual needs of people in the Third World?

13 What is the Third World? Which term is preferred for it?

14 What is 'well-dressing'?

15 How does well-dressing show a positive attitude towards Creation?

16 Why do Christians believe that they should care for the world?

17 List two environmental problems and two possible solutions.

18 Explain what one Church teaches about care for the world.

19 Why do some Christians become vegetarians?

20 List the conditions of the 'just war' theory.

21 What is a 'holy war'?

22 State one teaching of Jesus about war or violence.

23 State two arguments that a Christian might use *against* nuclear disarmament.

24 State two arguments a Christian might use *for* it.

25 What is the 'arms trade'?

WORKSHEET 4.15

Word list: Global issues

Environment

Acid rain   Rain with a high concentration of pollutants

Conservation   Preventing things going bad/looking after natural environment

Creation   The making or origin of the world

Ecology   The study of life in relation to its environment

Eden   Biblical garden in the Ancient Near East, supposed site of creation of human beings

Environment   Our surroundings (in this case the natural world)

Ex nihilo   'Out of nothing' – of Creation by God

Extinct   (Of wildlife) no more, died out entirely

'Green' issues   Issues concerned with caring for the Earth

Harvest Festival   Annual celebration of the good gifts of the Earth

Natural resources   Things that we use which are found naturally (e.g. oil, gas)

Ozone layer   Protective layer above Earth, absorbing radiation

Pollution   Rubbish and waste creating a mess in the world

Responsibility   Expectation (e.g. by society) that you will do something good

Stewardship   Looking after/caring for something that is not yours

Money

Absolute poverty   So poor that you have nothing of what you need to survive

Malnutrition   Not having enough food of the right kind and therefore being ill

Materialism   Worshipping wealth and money

Relative poverty   Being poor compared to others

Wealth   Having lots of money or goods

War and peace

Armaments   Weapons

Arms race   Countries building up stocks of weapons to ensure that they can match up to others

Conscientious objector   Someone who refuses to fight because of their beliefs

Conscription   Being ordered to join a force by law

Conventional weapons   Armed men, armed tanks, ships and aircraft, usually used to contrast with nuclear weapons

Defence   Protection of a country from invasion

Disarmament   Getting rid of weapons, especially nuclear ones

Holy war   War fought with the belief that God is on your side, or wants the fighting

Just war   War judged to be right, justifiable

Justice   Fairness

Military   Things (armies, weapons) concerned with war and defence

Multilateral   Action taken by all or a number of countries

Nationalism   Being proud of your country, putting it first

Necessary evil   Belief that although war causes suffering, it can sometimes be right to prevent more suffering or evil

Nuclear weapons   Weapons of mass destruction causing radioactive explosion and contamination

Oppression   Where one group or person mistreats another whom they have power over

Pacifism   Belief that war is always wrong

Persecution   Heavy oppression of one or many people

Refugee   Person who has left home and country and fled to another

Retaliation   Fighting back

Treaty   An agreement between countries that they will do certain things for each other

Unilateral   Action taken by one country

Christianity in today's world Teacher's Resource Book

UNIT 5

Arguments about God

This unit is quite different from the other four in that it deals with theological issues. They are securely rooted in human life, and in 'the big questions' that all people, and perhaps especially the young, ask about the meaning of life and the nature of God; nevertheless it is important that students are prepared for the change of pace.

It is our experience that young people enjoy talking about God. They may not use the correct technical terms (although these need to be encouraged for the examination), but they enjoy a good philosophical discussion. The fascinating thing about this part of RE is that even the student who has learning difficulties and will struggle to gain even a lower GCSE grade, can have a view on God. The role of the RE teacher is to help each of the students to articulate his/her view, along with others that they have been exposed to, on paper or in some other medium for the examination.

Theology is one of the oldest academic disciplines but ultimately all worthwhile discussion of God arises out of everyday experience. People's ideas about God are subject to and revised by their life experiences. Theology is not a theoretical discipline but the religious answers people arrive at to the questions that confront them in their world today. So this unit needs to be considered in the light of all that has gone before concerning real-life dilemmas in which Christians find themselves, which affect, and are affected by, their ideas about God.

Overview

There is a progressive structure to this unit which should be borne in mind, particularly if you decide to use the unit in a different order.

The first two investigations open up the question: does God exist? – 5.1 considers in overview why some people believe in God; 5.2 then develops this in more detail, looking at three of the most common reasons people give for their belief, namely the origins of the universe, the design of the natural world, and personal religious experience.

Of course the existence of God cannot really be proved, so the rest of the unit pursues the lines: supposing God does exist, what is God like? (5.3); how is God known? (5.4); why does God allow suffering? (5.5).

The final investigation (5.6) looks at life after death and also reviews many of the themes earlier in the book.

Starting strategies

Page 89

As in previous units the title page offers a discussion as a starting point. **Worksheet 5.1** uses the cartoon.

However, there are other possible ways into this unit. For example:

1 A simple brainstorm (as a class, in groups or even as individuals) of the word **God** will raise all sorts of issues and ideas, which the teacher can then develop in whatever way suits the class best. It may be that this initial brainstorm determines in what order the spreads in this unit will be tackled – the class deciding with the teacher what they need to sort out first.

2 The initial brainstorm can lead to second (or even third) stage work, by highlighting all the words that are descriptions of God as opposed to those that are phenomena associated with God. It is useful at this stage if the teacher can manage to use the word God in the neutral sense (until a discussion of Christian teaching begins).

3 A third stage might look at positive and negative images of God, or at Christian versus secular ways of seeing God, or at anthropomorphic versus transcendent images, and so on.

Other resources

Videos are another, rather more impersonal, way into the unit (this may be appropriate in some settings). The BBC *Taking Issue* programme *Does God Exist?* is helpful, and there is an old ITV *Believe it or Not* programme called *One God?* which is quite useful as an introduction to a variety of religious responses, from which Christianity can be selected.

It may be helpful to introduce students to the book *Sophie's World* by Jostein Gaarder (arguably the most surprising bestseller of the 90s) if they do not already know it. This is about a young girl who is befriended by a philosopher who gives her a crash course in the history of philosophy. It is also very helpful for teachers as a summary and has some useful sections in which Sophie argues with the philosopher about many of the issues tackled in Unit 5. Particularly helpful sections in the book include: the introduction to what philosophy is (pages 11–13 of the paperback edition); the natural philosophers (pages 27–8); Jesus (pages 131–3) and the Creed (page 136); and the chapters on Darwin and the Big Bang. An extract is given in the notes below.

5.1 Why do people believe in God?

This investigation is a general introduction to a variety of broad reasons for belief. Don't get stuck in it for too long – it is meant as a survey which leads to the detailed teaching that follows.

In the discussion bear in mind that some of the stated beliefs will be held by members of your class. Class discussion needs to establish from the start a climate of sensitive exchange of opinions without ridicule.

Page 90
ACTIVITY You can develop this into a more mobile and interactive task. Clear the centre of the room of furniture if possible. Sit students around the edge. Draw a line down the middle of the room. In carpeted rooms use string! Put a label at one end 'There is a God for sure' and at the other 'There is definitely no God'. Students are invited to place their name (on a slip of paper) on the line where they feel their current belief is best represented. It is important to explain that this is a snapshot of how they feel about God at that time, and that their positioning might change another day.

Students are then invited to comment (without being personal) on the spread of names (every class will have a different pattern) and then to ask if there is anyone who wants to explain why they put their name where they did. This will lead to a general discussion, after which students should be allowed to move their name if they feel that it is appropriate in the light of discussion.

A homework exercise might be to write about what happened during the lesson from their own point of view.

SAVE AS . . . Worksheet 5.2 provides a writing frame to help less able students to write an essay in response to this question.

Page 91
FOCUS TASK Worksheet 5.3 provides a copy of the table for students to fill in.

SOURCE H Worksheet 5.4 is a homework sheet which probes this argument in more detail since it does not get a detailed airing in the next investigation.

5.2 Can you prove that God exists?

The three arguments studied in this unit – *origins of the universe* (pages 92–3), *design* (94–5), and *experience* (98–9) – are those specified in NEAB Syllabus D. Others could be tackled if time allows.

The viewpoints included are constrained by the space available and the need to make this subject matter manageable. Writing about these topics has probably used up more paper over the centuries than any other! You may well have favourite examples or sources to add.

The spread on religious experience (pages 98–9) is taken from the charismatic Anglican tradition. You could easily use another story from another tradition as the basis for the investigation. You will almost certainly be able to invite in a Christian who would be willing to talk about their own, different, experiences. It might be particularly interesting to invite in a monk or a nun who could talk about their personal experience of God.

The 'interlude' (pages 96–7) about interpretations of

Genesis 1 and 2 is designed to aid students studying syllabuses which call for a consideration of the scientific response to religion.

Page 92
This same diagram is used in Focus Task B on page 99 as the basis for recording students' work on the whole investigation. **Worksheet 5.5** provides a simplified version more suited to the task.

This visual can be used as the basis for display work, e.g. a poster summarising the arguments for and against each. Such display work has a deep purpose. With an examination looming, the thought that has to go into students' organisation of their ideas, building their conceptual understanding into a chart or diagram, is an ideal way of firming up their grasp of the content.

Pages 92–3
Argument 1: Origins of the universe
This argument is also known as the 'cosmological argument'.

Sophie's World has a passage which could help students debate with this First Cause argument:

> *Where does the world come from?*
> *She hadn't the faintest idea. Sophie knew that the world was only a small planet in space. But where did space come from?*
> *It was possible that space had always existed, in which case she would not also need to figure out where it came from. But could anything have always existed? Something deep down inside her protested at the idea. Surely everything that exists must have had a beginning? So space must sometime have been created out of something else.*
> *But if space has come from something else then that something else must also have come from something. Sophie felt she was only deferring the problem. At some point, something must have come from nothing. But was that possible? Wasn't that just as impossible as the idea that the world has always existed?*
> *They had learned at school that God created the world. Sophie tried to console herself with the thought that this was probably the best solution to the whole problem. But then she started to think again. She could accept that God had created space but what about God himself? Had he created himself of nothing? Again there was something deep down inside her that protested. Even though God could create all kinds of things, he could hardly create himself before he had a 'self' to create with. So there was only one possibility left: God had always existed. But she had already rejected that possibility! Everything that existed had to have a beginning.*
> *Oh drat!*
> *Who had jolted Sophie out of her everyday existence and suddenly brought her face to face with the great riddles of the universe?*

Sophie's World, Jostein Gaarder (Phoenix House, Orion Publishing Group)

Pages 94–5

Argument 2: The design of the natural world

The second argument is known as the 'teleological argument'.

Almost all past philosophers have engaged with this argument. David Hume is the most notable one that we have omitted. He identified four main problems with the design argument:

1 We do not know the way the world was made and we cannot deduce that cause and effect apply in the same way as processes we have observed.
2 Why do we think this world is perfect? It's the only one we know. But maybe in comparison with other worlds of which we do not know it's a botched job!
3 Who designed the designer?
4 Why is the world so full of evil?

A very different way to get students to share their ideas about the design of the natural world would be a 'guided fantasy', although teachers should be wary of introducing such techniques unless they are sure that the class can deal with them sensibly. If you want to try then here is a rough plan. Relax the class and encourage them to sit comfortably without disturbing anyone else. Then talk them through the following:

'Be still and quiet. It will probably help to close your eyes so that you are not distracted by anything else. As you sit still, become aware of your own breathing and the rhythm of your heartbeat. Sink into yourself as you listen and relax.

Imagine that you are leaving the room in which you are sitting and going on a journey. You may travel far or just a short distance. You find yourself in beautiful countryside. It is sunny and still with a slight breeze in the trees.

Look around, take in the colours, the sights, the smells, the sounds. Stop to soak it all in.

As you look around you become aware that you are not alone. There are many creatures around you. Some are tiny, others very large. Look at them, touch them if you dare. On this visit you do not see any other people.

When you are ready look up and be ready to answer the question: who or what was responsible for all that you saw?'

Pages 96–7

Interlude: How do Christians interpret Genesis 1 and 2?

It is important that students understand that, contrary to popular belief, there is actually very little dispute in the minds of many Christians between science and religion. Nor was there in the past. Darwin and others have often been misrepresented as being anti-Christian. This was not so, and today there are many eminent scientists who have a deep and meaningful faith in God. For these people, science helps them to see even more powerfully the amazing nature of the God who is at the root of all

things. Indeed science can help to enhance religion and vice versa – the two are inter-dependent rather than opposed.

It has been said that there are really only two necessary subjects on the school curriculum – Science, which asks *How* things work, and Religion, which asks *Why*. It might be interesting to get students to set up a debate along these lines, possibly involving the school Science Department.

More able students might also benefit from having a deeper discussion of these issues with local university students, or with carefully selected members of the Christian faith community.

A helpful video on this topic might be the CEM production: *The Question Is*. This contains four 20-minute videos which explore the interaction of science and religion and will stimulate students of average and above ability to think about these issues.

Page 97

Question 5 The page references are to: (14) the sanctity of all life as created by God; (36) the centrality of human relationships to God's Creation; (76) the role of humans as God's appointed stewards. There are many powerful ideas in these passages. As an extension exercise ask your students to read and mark a copy of Genesis 1–3 (or, if you need to select a smaller part, 1.24–2.4 and 2.15–3.20) to identify other central ideas or 'eternal truths'.

Pages 98–9

Argument 3: Religious experience

In case you're wondering, all the smiley people were not set up – we asked each for a picture and these were what we got!

Page 99

FOCUS TASK A Clearly this task will lead to discussion not only on the nature of experience but on the specific of 'Does God heal people today?'. Christians do not agree about this. Not all Christians would accept John Rajah's story as a miraculous intervention by God. In the Bible God heals people – in the Gospels there are more than 30 stories of Jesus healing people – but Christians vary as to whether this sets a precedent for today. If you wish to explore this in more detail, here are the three main views:

1 Jesus did not physically heal people. He dealt with emotional or spiritual problems.
2 Jesus did heal people. But things like that do not occur today. Jesus' healing work has been taken over by modern medicine.
3 God is unchanging. God healed people in biblical times. What God did then, God can and will still do today.

FOCUS TASK B This reviews the last four spreads.
Worksheet 5.6 helps with task 5 by guiding less able students through writing an essay about these arguments.

Worksheet 5.7 provides examination practice on the same topic – arguments about the existence of God.

5.3 What is God like?

The first spread explores students' images of God. The second (pages 102–3) focuses on language about God (one of the more difficult areas of NEAB Syllabus D for students to grasp is the dichotomy between God as personal or impersonal, immanent or transcendent). The third spread (pages 104–5) deals with the Trinity and then the final spread (pages 106–7) investigates Jesus in more detail (which is required for some syllabuses).

Pages 100–101

SOURCES A–D Expressing ideas about God in pictures might appear to some to be blasphemous and if so it would certainly not be appropriate to use this spread. However, the idea is to encourage students to use images as way into expressing their ideas about God. Certainly the discussion should lead into an awareness that all images (just like all descriptions of God) are attempts to express the inexpressible. They might reflect one small aspect of the character of God, but it is impossible to see all of God's aspects at once.

You could ask students to draw their own ideas about God *before* introducing the spread in the book.

Pages 102–3

Personal or impersonal? Immanent or transcendent?

The examination may well test whether students know the meaning of the words personal and impersonal, immanent and transcendent. It is also important for students to be aware of these ideas as they study Christian beliefs in Jesus as the incarnate Son of God and the concept of the Trinity. **Worksheet 5.8** is a support sheet on this topic.

Worksheet 5.9 investigates the different qualities we ascribe to God through an alphabet of God's qualities. If students are stuck here are some ideas:

Amazing	**N**ever-ending
Beautiful	**O**mnipotent
Compassionate	**P**eace
Daring	**Q**uiet
Equitable	**R**ighteous
Fearsome	**S**ilent
Generous	**T**olerant
Helpful	**U**nselfish
Invisible	**V**iolent
Just	**W**ar like
Kind	e**X**traordinary
Life-giving	**Y**outhful
Mighty	**Z**ealous

Page 103

FOCUS TASK You could gather other prayers for students to consider in task 3. You could even, if appropriate, probe your students' own experience of prayer. Many students have prayed at some time. Get them to write on a slip of paper about any occasion they have prayed. Make sure they keep it anonymous. Then use the completed papers to draw up a class 'spider' diagram showing the reasons people prayed and the types of prayers they prayed.

Pages 104–5

The Trinity

Question 1 You could present this question as a three-cornered or triangular diagram similar to the background of page 104. You could also include the Apostles' Creed (Source N on page 106) in the exercise. As an extension for more able students you could give extra Bible references to work with, e.g. *Father:* Genesis 1.1–5; *Son:* Mark 1.45 and 15.33–41; *Spirit:* John 14.16 and Romans 5.8.

FOCUS TASK Worksheet 5.10 supports this task.

Pages 106–7

Jesus

SOURCE N At Christian confirmation classes (when people are preparing to become adult members of a Church) they often study the Apostles' Creed, line by line. Ask students to imagine they have to lead a confirmation class: 'What questions do you think people will have about it? Write the questions that you think people will have. In a different colour write the way you would answer them.'

Page 107

ACTIVITY B Worksheet 5.11 supports task 3 with a storyboard template.

FOCUS TASK If students need help with structuring this essay we suggest:

Paragraph 1 Explain the meaning of the quotation.
Paragraph 2 Explain why Christians might want to understand more about God and how they might do so.
Paragraph 3 Explain why Christians also believe God cannot be fully understood.
Paragraph 4 Reach your own conclusion as to whether you agree with St John and explain why.

St John Chrysostom is not to be confused with either of the St Johns in the Bible. Chrysostom means 'Golden-mouth' – he was a powerful speaker. As an Archbishop he tried to reform the Church, which made him unpopular and as an old man he was banished from the Roman Empire. He died of heat exhaustion on the long journey into exile.

5.4 One God ... revealed in many ways

This investigation has three self-contained spreads about different aspects of revelation, which could be used selectively in any order. The first spread (pages 108–9) introduces different modes of revelation which students will need to be aware of for their examination. It uses the (hopefully not too irreverent) metaphor of a theme park as a way in. The second spread (pages 110–11) looks at two contrasting examples of revelation: one to an individual and one to an entire tradition. The final spread (pages 112–13) looks at four contrasting kinds of religious experience: *conversion*; *charismatic experience*; *sacramental ritual*; and *prayer and meditation*.

Christians experience God in many different ways, for example in worship, in daily life, through one-off special experiences. It is important that students understand that there is no spiritual superiority to be gained through any of these experiences (although some believers may try to persuade them that this is so) and that all are equally valid. Christians may experience all, some or just one of them throughout their lives. These different experiences are all ways of coming to know God. One aim in this investigation is that students grasp the breadth of ways of 'knowing' God and that they understand 'know' does not necessarily mean to see or to talk with in the way that we 'know' people in everyday relationships. Rather we need to communicate to students the idea that the relationship between the believer and God is experienced in a variety of ways.

This investigation builds logically on the work on Jesus (pages 106–7) since Christians claim that Jesus makes God known to people.

Page 109
FOCUS TASK Worksheet 5.12 is a copy of the theme park illustration with space to write, for use with task 2.

Another way of using this spread is to survey the class or other classes in the school about which ways of knowing God they have tried out or would try out. **Worksheet 5.13** is a survey sheet for this purpose.

Pages 110–11

How do Christians find out the will of God?

ACTIVITY For task 1 you could help students by suggesting the following: prayer; the advice of other Christians; the Bible; Church teaching; human wisdom and insight; dreams; visions; God talking; circumstances; discussion with other Christians; worship; Bible study, etc.

Pages 112–13

Experiences of God

FOCUS TASK This may need reference back to students' work on religious experience (pages 98–9). The NEAB Syllabus D examination may ask questions about any of these forms of experience as illusion or reality.

The forms of experience selected are dictated by the syllabus but, as we have said above, this is a very selective list. Also, since we have aimed for brevity and clarity on a single spread, we have only given one highly selective example of each form of experience.

This approach makes Christian experiences seem self-contained. **Worksheet 5.14** works to counter this image as five different Christians describe their experiences.

Note that sacramental worship is more than just the

Eucharist. There are seven sacraments in the Orthodox and Catholic traditions: *Baptism*; *Confirmation* (or *Chrismation* in the Orthodox tradition); *Eucharist*; *Reconciliation* (confessing your sins to God); *Marriage*; *Sacrament of the sick* (anointing a very sick person with oil and praying for them); *Ordination* (being appointed a priest). Most Anglican Churches regard the first three of these as sacraments. Students could investigate more about other sacraments.

The four forms of experience presented should ideally be supplemented. Encourage your students, particularly your higher attainers, to extend their table in the Focus Task by looking at other forms of experience claimed by Christians. They could scour the Student's Book, other textbooks and information books for examples.

They could talk to a range of Christians. You could set up a panel of local Christians to talk about how they 'know' God, possibly in response to students' pre-prepared questions. The panel members and students would need to understand that there was no element of competition in this and that all had an open say and were not there to proselytise.

You could use video clips of people talking about their experiences of God. On network television, *Songs of Praise* and similar programmes, especially in the early Sunday morning slot, include many such interviews each week. Radio should not be ignored, either.

Music plays an important role in many Christians' experience of God. It isn't possible to reflect this in a textbook, but you might be able to do so in class. You could collect a variety of Christian music to play to students. They could research the origin of each, discuss which they prefer or find most helpful. What beliefs about God are expressed through the music? Through which form would God be most likely to speak to them? Easily available sources might include: traditional hymns, modern hymns or choruses, gospel music, liturgical music, Taize music, cathedral choirs, ethnic music, rock music, meditative reflective music. Much of this can be taped free from the television or radio, borrowed from local Christians, or from your local library, or (if you have funds) bought from a Christian bookshop. You could even go to a concert or a service to experience the music first hand.

You could ask the students to create their own 'Songs of Praise', putting together a wide range of music styles together with interviews with people who find that kind of music speaks to them.

Page 113
FOCUS TASK Task 4 opens up the controversy over new forms of worship, which is an active one in all traditions today – for example, the criticism by Robert Runcie (mentioned on page 102) who said that 'huggy feely, happy clappy worship had – with the overhead projector – reduced God to the status of a puppet'. You could discuss this in the form of a class debate if students have personal experience of either traditional ritualised worship or modern spontaneous worship. You could show videos of two contrasting services and ask students which they would prefer to go to and why.

Here is a possible summary task to bring together the work on the last three spreads.

'Imagine that some people have been raised on a desert island, knowing nothing about religious belief on this Earth except the first line of the Apostles' Creed, a copy of which has been miraculously washed their way: 'We believe in God . . .'. When they are rescued they want to find out more. Write the outline for a story in which they try to find out more. For your story decide whether and how the following things might help them in their quest: the natural world; the Bible; Church leaders; Christian worship; religious experience.'

Worksheet 5.15 provides a light-hearted way of reviewing the students' work on investigations 5.1–5.4.

5.5 Why do people suffer?

One of the most common questions that people raise is 'If there is a God then why does He allow suffering?'. It is the counter to the design argument. David Hare (Source J, page 91) expressed this most eloquently. It was also discussed on page 95. Now we return to this and investigate in detail how Christians explain the existence of suffering in this world and how they reconcile it with belief in an all-powerful God.

Pages 114–15 focus on the Dunblane massacre which was still powerfully in our students' minds at the time of writing. Pages 116–20 explore Christian perspectives on suffering and evil.

Throughout this investigation you will face the fact that students may want to tell their personal experiences of bitterness towards God: 'Why did God let my . . . die?'. There is obviously room for such discussion if it can be sensitively handled. However, in this investigation more than any other the mismatch between the Christian explanation of suffering (which must be understood for examination purposes) and their own feelings or beliefs might be most obvious.

Page 115
SOURCE C A possible strategy for students' overall work on this investigation is for them to prepare a radio broadcast. **Worksheet 5.16** suggests a structure for such a task.

Pages 116–17
Christian perspectives on suffering
SOURCE F You could ask students to design a symbol for each explanation of suffering.

5.6 What kind of future do Christians look forward to?

This final investigation has two purposes. First, to investigate Christian ideas about life after death (which appear on some syllabuses). Second, to pull together a range of themes from the unit. Pages 121–3 investigate ideas about heaven and hell. Page 124 focuses on the issue of salvation; page 125 on attitudes towards death; page 126 on the Kingdom of Heaven or the Kingdom of God.

There are a number of useful videos that might be used at this point in the course. The BBC series *Taking Issue*, Programme 2: *Life after Death?* is helpful, as is the *Words into Action* programme *Life and Death*. There is also an *RE Collection* programme on the same topic.

From time to time there are some useful programmes on television which it is worth taping. A BBC *QED* programme on near-death experiences would provide a useful stimulus for discussion about the afterlife – is it our expectations that determine what our afterlife will be?

It might be possible to ask a local funeral director to come into school and talk about his/her work. This has worked well in our experience, but it needs to be handled very sensitively and teachers must first try to ascertain whether any students might be upset due to recent bereavement.

Alternatively a local priest (or a Reader – is there one on the staff?) or minister, or others who take part in funerals and/or comfort the bereaved, may be useful people to ask in for students to interview (but do let them have the questions beforehand!). They could describe a typical funeral service: what elements it contains; what Bible passages are said; what prayers are used; what hymns are sung, etc.

Page 121
SAVE AS . . . It is our experience that young people want to talk about death, not out of a morbid fascination but from an interest in the unknown and yet inevitable.

Some interesting additional sources are on the BBC *Words into Action* programme *Life and Death*, e.g. Frances Domenica of Helen House Children's Hospice says: 'Death is a beginning not an end and the more often I'm present when someone dies the more strongly I believe that. I can't believe that when somebody's heart stops beating and they stop breathing that they cease to exist. Although we don't understand what is to come I'm convinced that there is something more than this life.'

Page 124
Who will go to heaven?
Question 2 *The Private Memoirs and Confessions of a Self-justified Sinner* by James Hogg is a story set in Edinburgh in the 17th century. The writer is met by the Devil in the form of a mysterious stranger, who persuades him that he is among the elect – God has chosen him to go to Heaven. The writer believes in predestination, i.e. that God has already chosen who will go to Heaven and who will go to Hell, and what you do in this life makes no difference.

The writer decides it is his duty to cleanse the world of all the sinners so that world is left to the righteous and the elect to enjoy. This leads him to commit many crimes, including the murder of his own brother. He believes that he is doing God's work. He is both increasingly appalled and increasingly obsessed by his crimes. In the end the Devil persuades him that he might as well kill himself, which he does. However first he writes a memoir explaining what he did and why he did it. This forms the main part of the book.

There is a long introduction to the book which pretends to be written by an editor who has found this long-lost memoir. It warns off others from giving in to the temptations that come from believing you are saved.

Page 126
Life before death

FOCUS TASK This task could be attempted by an adventurous teacher as a video, with groups presenting a modern version of the Sermon and linking it to topics covered in the morality sections.

Worksheet 5.17 provides two sheets of examination practice on Satan and life after death.

Page 127 provides end of unit review tasks; **Worksheet 5.18** is an end of unit test; **Worksheet 5.19** is a word list.

Conclusion
Pages 128–9
There are a number of things that students will need to know at the end of the course if they are to achieve a good grade in the examination. But we hope that students will also have got a good deal more from the course than an examination grade.

The final spread emphasises this. Hopefully each student will have been able to reflect more thoughtfully about important issues and will have learned to express their responses in a more coherent way which will prepare them for adult life.

Page 129
RE-EVALUATION You can re-use Worksheet 1.1 at this stage and compare the students' answers now with their answers at the beginning of the course. You could also return to Worksheet 5.2 for students to answer the final question again.

Worksheet 5.20 suggests a review and revision activity for the entire book. Students are now experts and they should be ready to interview a range of Christians about their views on a range of issues. The worksheet suggests questions but students could add their own. This will help with revision in that it will also force students to use some of the terminology and ideas they will need for their examination.

Arguments about God

Aren't the mountains wonderful? God made a beautiful world.

Did God also make the earthquakes and volcanoes that kill thousands of people every year?

Did God make the evil too?

I know God is there – I've felt a presence.

There is goodness in the world, so there must be a God.

It was all in your mind.

1 Study each of the arguments in this cartoon. What evidence do you think each speaker might use to support their view? Write their evidence in the boxes.
2 Which speaker do you most agree with? Explain your choice.

WORKSHEET 5.2

Theists, atheists and agnostics

Write an essay: **Why do people believe in God?**

Use this sheet to focus your thoughts and to organise your ideas. Words to use:

theists   atheists   agnostics

Return to your essay when you have reached the end of the unit, and add to the last part.

Some people are called t_____. They are certain that God exists. One reason they say that God exists is: _____

_____

_____

_____

Some people are called a_____. They do not believe in God at all. One reason they say God cannot exist is: _____

_____

_____

_____

Some people are called a_____. They are not sure whether God exists. One reason for their view is: _____

_____

_____

_____

I have looked at all of these ideas. I could be called a/an _____. This is because I believe: _____

_____

_____

_____

Date _____

Having now looked in more detail at the arguments used by theists, atheists and agnostics during this unit I would call myself a/an _____. This is because: _____

_____

_____

_____

Date _____

Reasons to believe

Why people believe in God	Examples	Why people do not believe in God	Examples
Science shows beauty and order in the natural world, which must have been created by somebody		Because of suffering, chaos and evil in the world	
Because I have 'experienced' God for myself		Because God is silent	
Because my parents or community have brought me up to believe in God		Because I dislike Christians I meet	
Because I am afraid of what might happen to me if I do not believe		Because science has disproved the basic beliefs of Christianity	

Christianity in today's world Teacher's Resource Book   © John Murray

Is belief in God a good 'insurance policy'?

Read this letter from an insurance company and then complete the response form for yourself, having considered their offer carefully.

A PERSONAL MESSAGE from *Paradise Insurance*

Dear student

Have we got news for you!

We are sure that you will not want to miss out on our fabulous WIN WIN offer . . .

Finding these philosophy lessons a bit confusing?

Atheist, Agnostic . . . don't even know how to spell them? Don't want to think about it at all??

Your worries are over! **The answer is right here! –**
Believe in God and cover all your options!!

It's so simple – just BELIEVE IN GOD ANYWAY . . . THEN . . .

 **IF GOD EXISTS THEN YOU WIN A PLACE IN HEAVEN WHEN YOU DIE!!**

 **IF GOD DOES NOT EXIST – SO WHAT? YOU WON'T KNOW ABOUT IT ANYWAY!!**

Dire warning! **If you do not believe in God, then you die and find that God does exist after all, you may earn yourself a ticket to . . . HELL!!**

The choice is yours . . .

This offer extends for a lifetime . . .

. . . but don't leave it until it's too late!!

To Paradise Insurance

Your offer is [please delete two]
GOOD/TEMPTING/UNACCEPTABLE.

I understand that you are offering me the chance to achieve happiness forever by

_____

_____

_____

_____

If I do not accept your offer, I understand that the penalty might be _____

_____

This is my choice:
I DO/DO NOT accept your offer because

_____

_____

_____

_____

Thank you for your kind offer!

Arguments why God might exist

Note to teachers:
You may wish to enlarge this to A3 when photocopying.

This is a simplified version of the diagram on page 92 of your book, for you to use with task B on page 99.

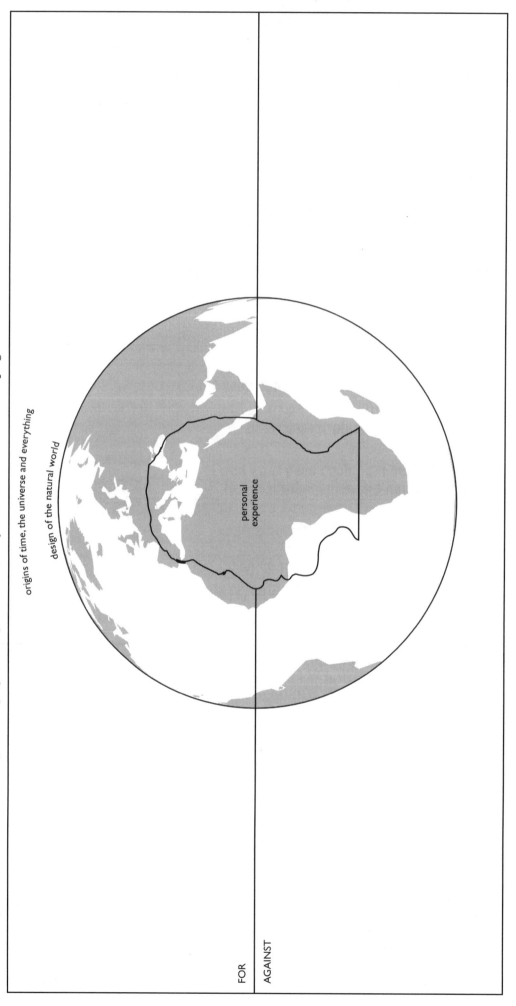

origins of time, the universe and everything

design of the natural world

personal experience

FOR

AGAINST

Christianity in today's world Teacher's Resource Book

© John Murray

WORKSHEET **5.6**

Does God exist? An essay

You have seen that people believe in God for a variety of reasons. Check you
have understood these arguments by re-reading pages 92–9 of your book, then
write an essay using these paragraphs to help you. You will need to add the
words in the box to complete the paragraphs *and* use your own words to explain
your own view.

Missing words:	Big Bang	healed	blood poisoning	experience	Paley	watch	thumb
	origin	First Cause	accident	God	design	God exists	vision

In this essay I am going to investigate three arguments people use to prove that God exists.

Some people look to the _____ of the universe to prove that God
exists. They say that God is the _____ _____
of everything. Scientists have argued that it was a _____ _____
which caused the universe to start off. Atheists say that this was started by an
_____, while Christians say that it was _____
who set it in motion.

Other people look to _____ in the universe to prove that God
exists. Some use the example of the human _____ to show that
there is design behind all things. A man called _____ also used the
_____ to prove this point.

Still other people say that it is their _____ of God which makes
them believe that he exists. One man, John Rajah, had _____
_____ and was seriously ill. He had a _____
and as a result began searching for God. He was _____ when
some Christians prayed for him. His experience convinced him and his sister that
_____ _____.

My own view on these arguments is . . .

(In the final paragraph explain your view about each of the arguments, whether they
convince you, or whether you see problems with them.)

Examination practice: Arguments about the existence of God

a) Give an account of a Creation story from a religious tradition. (6)

_____

_____

_____

_____

_____

_____

_____

b) Explain the argument for the existence of a Creator God based on:
   i)   what we know about the world,
   ii) what we know about the human body. (8)

   i) _____

_____

_____

_____

_____

   ii) _____

_____

_____

_____

_____

c) 'You can accept scientific theories about the origin of the universe and believe in a Creator God at the same time.'
Do you agree? Give reasons for your answer showing that you have thought about more than one point of view. (6)

_____

_____

_____

_____

_____

_____

_____

_____

_____

_____

_____

NEAB (GCSE short course) RE Syllabus D, Paper 1, 1997

WORKSHEET 5.8

An immanent and transcendent God

1 Complete this letter to God from a confused teenager.

Missing words: impossible   universe   Jesus   name   history   personal

Dear God

I just don't know what to make of you. Who really are you? What are you like? My friend says that you are very _____. She says that she talks to you just like she talks to me. My Gran says that you are the ruler of the _____. She always bows her head when she mentions your_____.

The young priest who comes into school to take our assemblies says that you have come into the world through _____ and that you have acted in _____. But one of my teachers says that you are above the whole world and _____ for us to understand or picture.

I don't know which one to believe. Maybe they are all a bit right in their own ways.

Best wishes anyway, whoever you are

2 Now suggest which of the four people mentioned understands God in which of these ways:

Personal _____

Impersonal _____

Transcendent _____

Immanent _____

An alphabet of God

Christians use many words to describe God because they need to think about
God's many different aspects.

1 Make up an alphabet of words used by Christians to describe God. Find one description beginning with each
   letter of the alphabet and write it on this sheet. You might do this for yourself, or look through the Bible for
   ideas, or ask a variety of Christians. Your teacher can also give you ideas.
2 Then for each word decide whether it suggests God is immanent, transcendent, personal or impersonal.
3 Compare your list with a partner's and discuss what have you found out from this activity.

		immanent	transcendent	personal	impersonal
A					
B					
C					
D					
E					
F					
G					
H					
I					
J					
K					
L					
M					
N					
O					
P					
Q					
R					
S					
T					
U					
V					
W					
X					
Y					
Z					

The Trinity

Use this writing frame for the Focus Task on page 104.

My chosen image is _____

which shows _____ .

The Christian belief in the Trinity means that _____

_____

_____ .

God the Father is _____

_____

_____ .

The artist has shown this by _____

_____

_____ .

God the Son is _____

_____

_____ .

The artist has shown this by _____

_____

_____ .

God the Spirit is _____

_____

_____ .

The artist has shown this by _____

_____

_____ .

The life of Jesus: Storyboard

Use this sheet with Activity B, question 3, on page 107.
Look up the Bible references given in your book, then use pictures and speech bubbles to complete the story strip below:

1 Jesus preaches – the crowds are amazed	**2** Jesus does miracles – people flock to see him
3 Jesus rides into Jerusalem – his friends do not know that within a week he will be dead	
4 Jesus has a meal with his friends – this will be his last	**5** Jesus dies on the cross – is this the end?
6 Jesus' tomb is found empty – he has been raised to new life	

Christianity World of Revelation

Use the text on pages 108–9 of your book to write your own descriptions of how each 'ride' at this 'theme park' can reveal God.

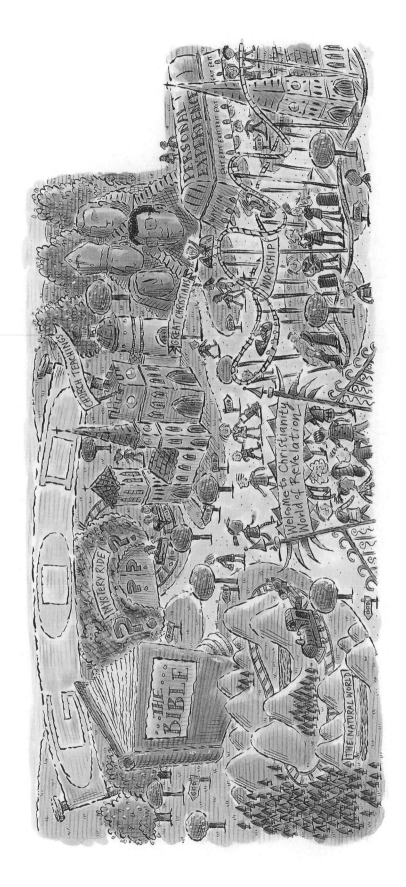

WORKSHEET 5.13

Knowing God questionnaire

1 Ask ten people about their views on these ways to know God.

Which if any have they tried?
Which if any would they like to try?
Which if any do they think is the most important?
Would they add any other way to know God?

Type of revelation	What people say about it
Natural world	
The Bible	
Church teachings	
Christian leaders	
Worship	

2 Use your table for a class discussion of the most common ideas about how to get to know God.

Christianity in today's world Teacher's Resource Book © John Murray

WORKSHEET 5.14

Experiences of God

Pages 112–13 make religious experiences seem very self-contained. In fact it is not like that. Many of these experiences merge into one another. Read the accounts below and try to classify them according to whether they are: **conversion**; **charismatic phenomena**; **sacramental ritual**; or **prayer and meditation**.

David:

One week I had missed Eucharist because I was on holiday. I went to another church, a Methodist church. It was a good service. In some ways it was much better than my traditional Anglican Liturgy. But at the end of it all I was empty. The words were fine, and the music was fine, but I needed something more concrete than just words. So I went to the nearby church for a Eucharist and it was what I needed. The bread and wine are my focus. I need the concrete and you can't get more concrete than bread and wine.

David, an Anglican

Michael:

I like the whole pattern of Orthodox Church worship . . . it brings together all the senses – sight, smell, hearing. You pray not only with your mind but with your body – when you make the sign of the Cross for instance or do a prostration. Church services have a rhythm to them. You can feel yourself moving along with its flow . . . it's like a ship. I could probably swim myself, and I might come ashore one day, but it would be much harder for me so I board a ship called the church and the church takes me along with it. It carries me much faster and with great force and I rejoice with the other people on board.

Michael, a member of a Russian Orthodox Church in London who works in the computer industry

---

Mike:

I sat at home at night and started reading the New Testament. I began to discover this person Jesus. . . . A couple of months later I'd got to the end of John's Gospel, where Jesus is talking to the Apostles at the Last Supper, when I just began to cry. Where I come from in Liverpool, big boys don't cry. I wasn't crying because I was sad. Something had touched me. I don't know if you call it God or what you call it. It was very real. Before that my faith had been very much my parents' faith, their understanding of Christianity. Mine's now moved on. It's different.

Mike, who went on to become a youth worker with the Emmaus Family of Prayer in the Catholic Diocese of Liverpool

---

Claire:

Vanya Moiseyev was an 18-year-old Russian Christian serving in the Communist Red Army. The official 'faith' of Communism was atheism. The army tried to force him to give up his Christian beliefs but he refused. This eventually led to his torture and murder by the Communist secret police. His body was found with a broken jaw, six stab wounds around his heart, severe bruising to his head and legs and burns on his chest.

My RE teacher gave me a book about Vanya Moiseyev when I was 15. I had always believed in God even though my family were not religious, and I was beginning to realise that just believing in God was not enough. If God really did exist I needed to admit my beliefs and tell others about this wonderful God. The story of Vanya's life and death made a huge impact on me at that time, because this young Russian, only a few years older than me, had stood up to powerful officials because he believed in the same God as me and lost his life doing so.

Claire, a member of a house church, who is now an RE teacher

Father Desmond:

A special moment for me happened during a Catholic Eucharist Congress in 1976 . . . There was a 'charismatic' Mass. Several of us chatted about going then everyone else dropped out so I went on my own. I found a seat at the end of the row so that I could get away quickly if I didn't like what was happening. What I was expecting was just an ordinary Mass. What happened was something that has totally changed my life. A lot of charismatic gifts [see page 112] were expressed during that celebration. After Communion there was what some Christians would describe as an altar call: 'If you have not yet given your life to the Lord Jesus you can do it now.' That sort of thing. I thought, 'Well Lord, I don't know what this is all about, but yes, I do want to give my life to you.'

. . . Those events were a real turning point. It made religion much more personal for me. At the centre was a personal relationship with the Lord and knowing that that was the most important thing. The rules and regulations were there to help support that not the other way round.

Father Desmond Seddon, a Catholic priest in Liverpool

WORKSHEET 5.15

God: A job description

This is one way of reviewing your work on what Christians believe about God.

When people start a job they may be given a job description which explains exactly what the job requires of them. It is often split up into sections. Now that you have spent some time considering different ideas about God, try to write a job description for God.

You could bring in ideas from earlier units but investigations 5.2, 5.3 and 5.4 will be particularly useful.

You might consider how different Christian traditions would complete the job description.

Main responsibilities:

1) concerning the world:

2) concerning people:

3) concerning life in general:

Key characteristics:

Method of communication with others:

Accountable to:

WORKSHEET 5.16

A radio broadcast about suffering

It is the week after the Dunblane massacre. You have to prepare a radio broadcast which responds to this event from a Christian standpoint. Record ideas for the broadcast as you work through pages 114–20 of your book.

The Dunblane incident

The book of Job

Other Bible passages

Christian writers

Other ideas, e.g. poems, hymns, interviews . . .

WORKSHEET 5.17

Examination practice: Satan and life after death

1 'Earth to earth, ashes to ashes, dust to dust.' (Alternative Service Book)

  a)   **i)**   What is usually happening when these words are said?

      ii) What might some Christians mean when they talk about purgatory? (8)

i) _____

_____

ii) _____

_____

_____

_____

_____

_____

  b)   Explain why some Christians think that the way they live will affect what happens to them after death. (7)

_____

_____

_____

_____

_____

_____

_____

_____

  c)   'No one knows what will happen when they die so it is not worth thinking about.'
Do you agree?
Give reasons to support your answer and show that you have thought about different points of view.
You must refer to Christianity in your answer. (5)

_____

_____

_____

_____

_____

_____

_____

MEG (GCSE short course) RE Syllabus B, Paper 2, 1997

WORKSHEET 5.17 (continued)

2 a) i) What is meant by the name 'Satan' (or the 'Devil')?
       ii) What do some Christians believe about the work of Satan? (8)

   i) _____
       _____

   ii) _____
       _____
       _____
       _____
       _____
       _____

   b) Explain why both the death and resurrection of Jesus are important to Christians. (7)

       _____
       _____
       _____
       _____
       _____
       _____
       _____

   c) 'Satan does not exist, it is people who are evil.'
       Do you agree?
       Give reasons to support your answer and show that you have thought about different points of view.
       You must refer to Christianity in your answer. (5)

       _____
       _____
       _____
       _____
       _____
       _____
       _____

MEG (GCSE short course) RE Syllabus B, Paper 2, 1997

End of Unit Quiz: Arguments about God

Test yourself or your neighbour with this quick quiz.

1 What is a *theist*?

2 Give three arguments for God's existence.

3 Give three arguments against God's existence.

4 What did Thomas Aquinas suggest?

5 What is the Big Bang theory?

6 What did Newton suggest showed that people are unique?

7 Who used the watch as an example of design?

8 With what was Epicurus concerned?

9 Briefly explain Darwin's theory.

10 Explain the sorts of truth found in Genesis.

11 What different questions do science and religion ask?

12 What do the following words mean when applied to God: *immanent, transcendent, personal, impersonal*?

13 Suggest one Bible passage which tells Christians that God is personal.

14 What do Christians mean by the Trinity?

15 What is meant by the *incarnation* of Jesus?

16 What is the difference between special and general revelation?

17 What was Vatican 2, and why was it important in the Catholic Church?

18 What are sacraments?

19 How may sacraments help Christians to know God?

20 What is prayer?

21 What answer do some Christians give to the problems of suffering?

22 Which Old Testament character suffered a lot?

23 What different ideas do Christians have about the Devil?

24 What are the essential elements of a Christian funeral service?

25 What do Christians mean when they talk about *resurrection*?

Word list: Arguments about God

You need to know all of these words and their meanings.

Agnostic   Someone who is not sure what they believe about God

Atheist   Someone who does not believe in God

Charismatic worship   Worship that emphasises the place of the Holy Spirit

Conversion   Changing in some way – used of becoming a Christian by personal choice

Cosmological   To do with the universe and Creation

Design   Order of a system which makes something work

Divine   About God or God-like

Eucharist or **Holy Communion**   Service recalling Jesus' last supper on Earth

Evil   Very bad things that happen

Evolution   Theory that the universe and all that is in it has developed over millions of years

Experience   Something that a person goes through

First Cause   Origin, what made something happen

Free will   God-given ability to live life as one pleases

Heaven   A state of being with God for ever

Hell   A state of being separated from God for ever

Immanent   (Of God) in the world

Impersonal   (Of God) distant, without human attributes

Incarnation   Jesus born as God in a human body

Meditation   To think deeply about something, in Christianity by focusing on God

Natural selection   Idea that nature fights against itself so that the fittest win and survive

Origin   Beginning, start

Parousia   Jesus' second coming/return to Earth

Personal   (Of God) like a friend, well known

Resurrection   Being brought back to life after death

Revelation   Making known

Sacraments   Rituals that express outwardly how a religious person feels inwardly

Satan   Evil personified

Sin   Disobedience towards God

Teleological   To do with design and purpose in the world

Theist   Someone who believes in God

Transcendent   (Of God) outside the world, separate from it

Trinity   Three persons in one being (God as Father, Son and Spirit)

WORKSHEET 5.20

Interview

You have found out a lot about Christianity. Now put your knowledge to use. To help to draw together all of the ideas that you have considered in this book, interview a Christian about his/her life and beliefs. Emphasise that the interviewee will be anonymous.

Use this sheet to record the responses.

Compare your results with those of others in the class. Have you found similar or quite different responses?

Write a paragraph on a separate sheet, explaining what you have learned from this exercise.

I How do you feel about God?
2 Have you experienced God? If so, how?
3 What makes you believe in God?
4 How does your faith affect your daily life?
5 What do you believe about life after death?
6 Does this belief affect your daily life too?
7 How would you sum up what being a Christian means to you in one sentence?